CHRISTIAN HOLINESS

Biblical Foundations

&

Resources for Today

Barry L. Callen

Emeth Press
www.emethpress.com

Christian Holiness: Biblical Foundations & Resources for Today

Copyright © 2023 by Barry L. Callen
Printed in the United States of America on acid-free paper

All rights reserved. No part of this book may be reproduced or transmitted in any form or by any means, electronic or mechanical, including photocopying, recording, or by any information storage and retrieval system, without the written permission of the publisher, except where permitted by law. For permission to reproduce any part or form of the text, contact the publisher., P. O. Box 533 Jackson, Georgia 30233, www.emethpress.com.

Library of Congress Cataloging-in-Publication Data

Names: Callen, Barry L., author.
Title: Christian holiness : biblical foundations & resources for today / Barry L. Callen.
Description: Jackson, GA : Emeth Press, [2023] | Summary: "This book is a fresh examination of the meaning of holiness from within the Wesleyan-Holiness Tradition"-- Provided by publisher.
Identifiers: LCCN 2023010968 (print) | LCCN 2023010969 (ebook) | ISBN 9781609471910 (paperback) | ISBN 9781609471927 (kindle edition)
Subjects: LCSH: Holiness--Christianity. | Holiness churches--Doctrines.
Classification: LCC BT767 .C28 2023 (print) | LCC BT767 (ebook) | DDC 234/.8--dc23/eng/20230426
LC record available at https://lccn.loc.gov/2023010968
LC ebook record available at https://lccn.loc.gov/2023010969

Christian Holiness For Today's Church And World

	Pages
Foreword by Jim Lyon v	
Voices of Commendation vii	
Preface ix	

HOLINESS FOUNDATIONS

1. A Fresh Vision of the Holy
  Who Is the Holy God? 1
2. Pondering "Earthrise"
  Holy Creation & Re-Creation 11
3. Providence or Politics?
  Guided by a Holy Hand 19

HOLINESS DIMENSIONS

4. Let's Get Energized!
  Partaking of the Divine Nature 29
5. Travel the Whole Salvation Road
  Being Guiltless Isn't Enough! 37
6. Watch Your Language
  Live a Life of "Yes-ness".. 45
7. The Ultimate Diet
  The Bread of Life is Served! 53
8. Please Don't Call Me "Christian"!
  Is This an Unholy Label? 61
9. Surviving Upside Down
  Holiness Wins While Losing 69
10. Holy Tasks Done in Holy Ways
  Swords and Rockets? 77
11. Which Rules Am I To Live By?
  Replace Legalism with Love 85
12. Making Room for Others
  Be Holy By Being Hospitable 93

HOLINESS OUTCOMES

13. Assuring a Holy Church
   No Social Club, Political Party 101
14. A United Christ Community
   Holiness Enables Unity 109
15. Heaven's Eventual Population
   Holiness Is Where You Find It 117

Recent Resources 125
Books Referenced 127

Foreword

These pages are very important for today's church. Christian "holiness" is a central subject of the Bible and of the Christian life and mission. "Be ye holy as I am holy!" Holiness is based on the indwelling power of the Holy Spirit, the missing piece in most church development emphases today. The idea of a present, personal, empowering, and life-altering encounter with the Holy Spirit in complete surrender to God's will is rarely in the mix, let alone being the foundation stone. *This must change!*

This book prompts renewed attention to and provides extensive biblical resources for pastors and local churches to reclaim this key part of our experience as Christians on our knees and on mission. The teaching of the Church of God Movement which raised me up had a heavy focus on the Holy Spirit and Christian holiness, as had many other bodies in this great Wesleyan-Holiness tradition. Unfortunately, it usually was expressed in sweeping terms designed to frame believers individually rather than transform them into change agents in the secular world around us.

It's reported in Luke 4 that, when Jesus returned to his hometown of Nazareth, he stood up to read in the synagogue. He proceeded to define himself, his calling, and his ambition for his church of the ages. His reading from Isaiah should be the primary text undergirding today's definition of Christian discipleship. Here's the theme: "The Spirit of the Lord is upon me, because he has anointed me to bring good news to the poor. He has sent me to bring release to the captives and recovery of sight to the blind, to set free those who are oppressed."

The primacy of the Holy Spirit in the ministry of Jesus must also be ours. Pentecost is pivotal. *Holiness is the currency of God's kingdom.* Barry Callen's presentation properly calls us to challenge the convention of today's western "evangelicalism" and embrace instead a more radical, more biblical stance, personal and social re-creation of all life that only the Holy Spirit can bring. This is the Christian commission and there can be no success without it.

Christian mission fulfillment depends on the presence and dynamic of the Holy Spirit. **Read these pages carefully and live them boldly!**

—**Jim Lyon**, General Director of Church of God
  Ministries for the United States and Canada;
  President of the Global Wesleyan Alliance.

Christian Holiness is the presence of the Holy God activating new beginnings on behalf of the fullness of human life. The Holiness stream of Christianity runs wide and deep, central to the very being of God, basic to the Bible's revelation, and appearing globally in every century of church history. It now offers fresh hope for a struggling Christian community in the twenty-first century.

—Barry L. Callen, *The Holy River of God.*

VOICES OF COMMENDATION

Hear well this potent prophetic voice! Callen calls Christian leaders to receive and live Christian holiness, being contemporary by reflecting life in Christ by his Holy Spirit.
—John Mark Richardson, Executive Director, Wesleyan Holiness Connection

The church is searching for fresh biblical truth to provide insight and direction. Dr. Callen has brought just that. Every Christian should be on this journey of "Holiness."
—Ronald V. Duncan, Executive Director, the Global Wesleyan Alliance

Here's urgency and hope about a critical issue facing churches today. Pastors, teachers, and laypersons need biblical guidance for exploring a deeper walk with the Lord. Here it is!
—Dan Schafer, President, World Gospel Mission

Other voices are heard on the back cover.

CHRISTIAN HOLINESS

**The person who properly--
thinks, seeks, sets, acts.**

The person who thinks with the mind of Christ has the perspective of Christ's own Spirit. This person seeks whatever pleases the Spirit of the Lord and yearns to know where Christ's Spirit is at work. The person who sets his mind on the Spirit of Christ sees the world through Christ's eyes and seeks to be a part of what Christ is doing now in the world.

—Dennis Kinlaw, *The Mind of Christ*

There must be a true otherness from the world's distorted values combined with a radiant divine presence warming that world. Christian believers are to be formed into the image of Jesus Christ and become active agents of redeeming love. This is the core message of the Bible and the central challenge of today. An unholy church is no church at all!

Preface

An historic Christian document was produced in 2006 by a group of leaders representing the Wesleyan-Holiness-Pentecostal traditions of the Christian faith. Called the "Holiness Manifesto," it points to a crisis now being faced by Christianity in North America and elsewhere.

This Manifesto reports that "the power and health of churches have been drained by the incessant search for a better method, more effective fad, and newer and bigger program to yield church growth." The sad result has been that "our people have become largely ineffective and fallen prey to a generic Christianity that results in congregations indistinguishable from the culture around them."

The purpose here is not to belabor this problem or analyze its several causes. It's enough to repeat the following as a sample of what somehow must be reversed:

> Holiness churches have tried so hard to keep up with generic "evangelicalism" for the sake of numerical growth that they have sacrificed their distinctive call to preach holiness throughout the land. Indeed, in a culture of consumerism, preaching what people want to hear is much easier than preaching the cost of discipleship. In this kind of milieu, the optimism inherent in the Wesleyan-Holiness message has been muffled.[1]

The entire biblical revelation calls us to pursue life, the journey from holiness lost to holiness regained.

Christian "spirituality" is the quest, under the direction of the Spirit of Jesus, for a recovered holiness. It's the pursuit of life lived to the

---

[1] Diane Leclerc, *Discovering Christian Holiness.*

glory of God out of obedience to the Spirit of God, who inspired and enables the quest and directs to its destination. The entire biblical narrative recounts the journey from original holiness to lost holiness to God's initiatives to recover the lostness.[2]

The Message of the Manifesto

This 2006 Manifesto went on to describe the distinctive message of the Christian gospel that is common to all denominational bodies comprising the traditions involved with the Manifesto.[3] This message is understood by them to be fundamental to the biblical revelation and essential for the well-being of today's church. It's a central answer to its contemporary struggle of the churches. A brief synopsis of this key message is offered.

"God is holy and calls us to be a holy people. God has abundant and steadfast love for us. God's holy love is revealed to us in the life and teachings, death and resurrection of Jesus Christ. God continues to work, giving life, hope and salvation through the indwelling of the Holy Spirit, drawing us into God's holy, loving life. God transforms us, delivering from sin, idolatry, bondage, and self-centeredness, and drawing us instead to love and serve God, others, and be stewards of creation."[4]

According to the Manifesto, one specific action needed today is to "preach the transforming message of holiness." A disturbing observation, however, came out the 2022 meeting of the Steering Committee of the Wesleyan Holiness Connection, the network that has grown out of the study process that produced the Manifesto years before. Leaders of the very denominations expressing the concern and calling for renewed preaching about holiness reported this. Many of their own preachers these days *are rarely preaching about holiness*!

It's an ironic fact. Passionate exhortations to pursue Christian holiness are barely heard in most churches. There's plenty of talk

---

[2] Barry L. Callen, *The Living Dead.*
[3] See Barry L. Callen, ed., *The Holy River of God.*
[4] The Manifesto and a series of essays explaining various dimensions of Christian holiness are found in Don Thorsen and Barry Callen, eds., *Heart & Life: Rediscovering Holy Living.*

about sin and encouragement for decent behavior. One concerned leader insists that too many sermons are self-help mini-seminars on becoming a better you. "I'm talking about the failure of Christians, especially younger generations, and especially those most disdainful of 'religion' and 'legalism,' to take seriously one of the great aims of our redemption and one of the required evidences for eternal life--*our holiness*."[5]

Christian holiness is not just about a *better* you but a *new* you, new in the image of Christ as enabled by the Spirit.

Various reasons are being offered for this failure of a holiness emphasis, some even more strident than the claim that sermons are being reduced to self-help seminars. One reason insists that the deeper issue is the wayward message coming from many pulpits, a gospel of "inclusion and diversity." It supposedly originated in seminaries that have created a generation of "theologically vacuous clergy pandering an easy-believism from the pulpits."[6] Other reasons originated from holiness church bodies themselves that allowed holiness teaching to deteriorate into "legalistic perfectionism, the supposed eradication of sin, a preoccupation with instantaneous holiness, and a privatizing rather than a holistic and socially constructive understanding."[7]

Whatever the several reasons, the result has been an unacceptable vacuum that must be addressed. These pages seek to provide relevant, biblically affirmed, and theologically responsible teaching, preaching, and devotional resources aimed at addressing this failure. The great truths about God's very nature, *holy love*, and God's central intention for his people, *holiness*, must be sounded forth again with clarity and power. The church's integrity and the power of its witness are at stake.

---

[5] Kevin DeYoung, *Hole in Our Holiness*.
[6] David Virtue, *The Seduction of the Episcopal Church*.
[7] Don Thorsen, in *The Holiness Manifesto*.

No Time to be Silent!

If Jason Vickers is right, and I surely hope he is, Christians now live in a fluid time of great potential for the message of Christian holiness. A growing number of today's sociologists of religion are contending that secularism is dead. The postmodern West is teeming with religion because, in its frustrations and fears, our times have developed a growing openness to and active interest in the supernatural.[8] There is mounting desire today for encountering the sacred, the holy.[9]

There is an unacceptable gap between our love for the gospel and our love for godliness. Put another way, we are more anxious to bring people to Christ that encourage a matured Christlikeness in those who do believe. To put a spotlight on holiness is not mere pietism or mechanical legalism or rigid fundamentalism. It's the essential and enabled way of the intended Christian life. We who belong to Christ are called to become Christlike, to be holy as God is holy. That raises many questions, yes, and also opens many doors.

Three Key Assumptions. Given today's mounting desire for contacting the supernatural, this certainly isn't the time for Christian pulpits and classrooms and personal testimonies to be silent on the subject of Christian holiness! Three basic theological assumptions must be in place.

1. **In-Depth Experience.** Experiential knowledge of God makes one a participant with God. Grace can no longer be defined as a metaphysical gift independent of consciousness, such as election; but grace is a conscious encounter with God through Christ by the Holy Spirit to the hearts of human beings.[10]

2. **Love Is Central.** Love in the biblical and Hebraic sense is the deepest motivational focus of personality. It is that centering, organizing principle which gives direction to life. It cannot be coerced.[11]

---

[8] Barry L. Callen, *The Living Dead*.
[9] Jason E. Vickers, *Minding the Good Ground*.
[10] Randy Howard, Tony Richie, *Pentecostal Explorations for Holiness Today*.
[11] Mildred Bangs Wynkoop, *A Theology of Love*.

3. **An Enabling Grace**. God's "prevenient" grace makes the experience and love possible. This grace is the presence of the Holy Spirit, so that the sinful predicament into which we are born is not the only factor in our human situation. While being pulled negatively by original sin, there is a counter-balancing pull away from self-destruction. Our human will is enabled, not to save itself, but to move toward the God who is graciously moving toward us. We have free will only because we have been graced with it by the very presence of God.

Admittedly, words like Christian "experience," "election," and "prevenience" can be distracting and confusing as well as foundational. Another such word is "perfect." Christian holiness often has been defined as "being made perfect" or "perfected in love." The biblical word for "perfect" doesn't mean "flawless," but *"fulfilling its intended purpose."* That purpose is the love of God reigning within a human life so that life can be full and productive in God's kingdom. One result of holy individuals is that the church, the gathering of the "saints," can be spiritually healthy and united in modeling Christ to the world.

Here's a brief definition of Christian holiness that's consistent with the above assumptions. We are Christian "saints" of God when "we are living at our best, with all our energies focused, all our abilities alert and involved, doing what we were created to do, *love*."[12] That's Christian holiness, fulfilling God's intention for us by our being filled with love and allowing an overflowing of that love to bless the world.

The Intent of These Pages

These pages explore the several dimensions of Christian love-holiness, including its biblical foundations and eventual outcomes. May the trumpets sound again, encouraging the very life of God to enter and enthuse his people. May "holiness" become more than a confusing and neglected religious word. May we who believe in Jesus Christ move on down the holiness road with the ministering Spirit,

---

[12] Eugene Peterson, *The Hallelujah Banquet.*

being perfected in love and sent on the divine mission to a hungry, struggling, and waiting world.

Let's no longer stop short of all that God intends and makes possible. We can be "saved" *from* sin, yes, but also filled with divine love, becoming saved *to* mission in this world as a distinctive, passionate, and truly set-apart people of God. "Be ye holy even as I am holy," says the Lord! The many dimensions of Christian holiness, with samples of their biblical definitions and current applications, are found here. More are to be found in the recent two-volume set *A Year with Rabbi Jesus*.[13]

The holiness of God's people is always defined and determined by the holiness of God. Our holiness is to be seen as a reflection of God's. Furthermore, it is only when we get a glimpse of God's holiness that we begin to feel the force of the imperative laid on us: you shall be holy.

Stephen A. Seamands,
Holiness of Heart and Life.

---

[13] *A Year with Rabbi Jesus,* 2 vols., 2021 and 2022, by Barry Callen, Steve Hoskins, and Jonathan Powers (Emeth Press, Anderson University Press, and the 1901 Press of Trevecca Nazarene University).

A Fresh Vision of the Holy

Christian holiness is wholly dependent on the nature of the divine reality. Exactly who is God, and who then are we to be? We become able to glimpse our goal only by catching sight of God's intention. God is the One who says, "I *am* the Lord your God who brought you out of Egypt. I am the One who *is* and *has* (Ex. 20:1-17). Gaze gratefully on this holy, invisible One who has become visible through earthly actions to free and empower. God is our origin, our pattern, our resource, our destiny.

The Holy God is to be Reflected in Holy Humans.[1]
Christian Holiness is . . . Seeing the holy God.
Isaiah 53; Colossians 1

---

[1] See Hubert Harriman and Barry Callen, *Color Me Holy: Holy God, Holy People* (Aldersgate Press, 2013).

To be holy is to grasp the open hand of God and be led graciously to his glowing heart of love. We come to love God for God's own sake. In adoration, we forget ourselves and find bliss in God, something overwhelmingly beautiful, something that takes our frail breath away and gives us the fresh breath of the divine Spirit. We fall silent before the Holy One about whom we can't manage to speak adequately. We also speak joyously about this Holy One because we cannot be silent.

Who God really is controls who we are to be and how we are to act toward others as God's representatives. If God is seen as a big policeman in the sky, with a club in hand ready to punish any misstep we make, we can manage to fear, possibly even respect, but hardly love such a God. The revelation of God in Jesus Christ, however, makes all the difference. On the cross is so very different from club in hand!

If God is the high and holy loving Father, exactly like the Son in nature and purpose, then we can and will *love* God. Divine holiness, ultimate reality, pure love, is now God-revealed. This God, the only true God, is to be my model, my life challenge, my gracious resource, my ultimate destiny. Christian holiness is realizing in Jesus who God really is and yielding gratefully to who God then calls us to be in his image.

God Reaches, Risks, and Redeems. The holy God has planted, nourished, and now is harvesting a holy people. We who come to believe this in faith soon will be privileged to rule with God from age to age. God's absolute power has been employed on our behalf, not to overpower but to love, save, and partner with us for the redemption of ourselves and all others. God is the One who came to die in order that we might live alongside the ever-living One. O God, for all this, we can't help but love you!!

Through the centuries, Christian thought about God has been surprisingly complex.[2] Beginning biblically, however, it was quite simple. God said, "*You* shall be holy, for *I* am holy" (1 Pet. 1:16). Holiness is the divine nature and intention for us, his loved children.

---

[2] Barry L. Callen, *Discerning the Divine: God through Christian Eyes.*

A vision of the true God and God's central intentions is what the whole Bible is intending to convey.

Here's the vision's bottom line. Our great need is to be with the God who, in Jesus Christ, has shown a remarkable determination to be with us. Relating to God is increasingly to reflect the divine nature and goals in our own attitudes and actions. God is on a mission. Becoming like God sends us out as partners on that mission. The biblical authors are seeking to convey that God acts on our behalf in order that the divine nature and intentions can be known and then reflected by us. God's nature is congruent with the nature of God's consistent actions.

God is what God does. Rather than primarily to be known as perfect, unchangeable, wholly other, and timeless, the biblical emphases are on God as present, active, seeking relationships, and being voluntarily vulnerable to our human decisions. God enlists our input, not because it's needed, of course, but because God desires authentic, dynamic, mutually loving relationships with and then through us. That's who God is and how God does.

These basic biblical truths clarify what true holiness really is. God is love, and love reaches, relates, risks, and redeems, even through voluntary suffering. That old rugged cross outside Jerusalem reveals the heart of God and our calling to be God's obedient and sometimes suffering children. For a picture of God in action on our behalf, remember the sacrifice of Jesus on the cross and understand that God's very nature is *loving grace*.[3] That vision is of divine holiness changes everything!

Relationality Brings Responsibility. For wise Christian thinkers like John Wesley in the eighteenth century and Clark Pinnock in the twentieth, God is understood properly. As biblically revealed and reflected in their writings, God is not to be known *only* as Creator, Judge, and King, but also and even especially as Savior, Lover, and Friend. The emphasis is to be on *relationality* and a resulting human *response-ability*.

God enables our openness to the divine as the divine actively expresses an enabling openness to us. Rather than our "fearing" and

---

[3] Barry L. Callen, *God As Loving Grace*.

obeying a God who mechanically dominates and controls everything, we mere humans are being enabled by God to choose a life-transforming relationship with God, to love the God who is showering on us amazing love.

Some people fear that God would be weak and less than God if humans were enabled to make real life choices for or against God. Not so. God is so sovereign that divine choices are made according to the divine nature, uncoerced by nothing else. Because God's nature is compassionate love, God freely chooses to save the world, even if necessary through voluntary expressions of apparent "weakness" and risk (e.g., the divine Incarnation in Jesus).

God so loved that Jesus arrived among us as God with us. The arrival was not as conqueror on a mighty white horse, but as a helpless baby in a smelly animal stable. God came to where we are, as one of us, to relate to us lovingly and invite our free choice of relating in loving response to him. The pulsating heart of biblical revelation is just this, paradoxical and yet not at all contradictory.

The sovereign God who stands above all creation is also the compassionate God who stoops to significant and costly involvement with the creation. Why? For the sake of the creation's well-being. God comes low that we might rise high. God displays true holiness and calls us to such holiness as enabled by the divine Spirit. Since God makes our choices possible, we are responsible for the choices we make. The fundamental choice to be made is our response to the deepest desire of God—*be holy as I am holy!*

A vision of the holy and loving God, the engaging and interacting, the reaching and risking God, is basic to all biblical revelation and for all aspects of the intended Christian life. The New Testament says that God has created a chosen race (1 Pet. 2:9-10). Christ is head of this new creation, the church. It's called to accept the Spirit's ministry and thus become first-fruits of the coming new order of holiness experienced and expressed (Rom. 8:23; 2 Cor. 1:22, 5:5; Eph. 1:13-14).

Words of Majesty and Mystery. Colossians 1:15–20 is known as a "Christ hymn," lyrics surely known and likely sung by both the author and first readers of this Pauline letter. These are sacred words full of holy images and magnificent claims. No biblical words carry more mystery and majesty. If you want to focus on the heart of divine revelation that conveys massive spiritual meaning, here it is. Jesus is . . .

> the image of the invisible God, the firstborn of all creation; for in him all things in heaven and on earth were created, things visible and invisible, whether thrones or dominions or rulers or powers—all things have been created through him and for him. He himself is before all things, and in him all things hold together.

God is Creator and Lord of all that is, and the Son, Jesus, is God's embodiment now come among us to make clear that God is *for us*.

God has come to clear the guilt of past sin and guide us into a renewed holy relationship with the holy Father. Therefore, these huge truth meanings about the nature, activity, and will of God are not mere intellectual propositions to be entertained with the mind. To ever grasp them adequately, one must become one with them by relating in faith to them with all of life. To "know" is to walk with and risk for, not merely to think about.

This cosmic Christ, "head of the body, the church," intends that the church play a key role in the redemption of creation. It's to join Christ's ongoing holy mission. The church is to live in the power of Christ's resurrection (Col. 3:3-4), the dynamic of the coming new day. It's to know God as present and active, a loving sovereignty who is reaching for sanctified divine-human relationships and calling for our willing mission partnership in a holy cause.

The word "holy" echoes through all true language about God. "Ours is the holy God who issues a holy call for us to participate in a holy mission to create a holy newness. We come to know God as we respond in faith to God's call, move out in God's power on God's mission, and open ourselves continually to God's eternal newness. God is the dynamic One who shatters all rigidities. God is the moving One who defies all narrow conceptual confinements. God is the living One who abandons all dead religion."[4]

---

[4] Gilbert W. Stafford, *Theology for Disciples*.

Exploring Biblical Texts

Isaiah 53. The prophet announces a dramatic expectation. Soon there would be God's coming day, indeed a holy day, and it turned out to be the day of Jesus. He would come vulnerably, surprisingly, showing the loving nature of the sovereignty of his all-powerful and life-renewing Father. This Sovereign over all creation would come with a dramatic show of apparent weakness, yes, weakness. Only in knowing the suffering Son would we ever be able to know properly the Self-giving Father or be his true, his holy people in the world.

Self-sacrificing love is the fundamental character of God. God is intimately connected with the world, caring for it intensely, and actively committed to its good. God necessarily, by his very nature, is sensitive to the world and its free choices of self-destructive waywardness. God willingly suffers because of us and for us, intending such suffering to continue *through us* on behalf of others.

Colossians 1. The sovereign power reigning over heaven and earth is the power of love that now has been demonstrated so dramatically in the life, death, and resurrection of Jesus. In him all the fullness of God was pleased to dwell. To really know God, we must look carefully at Jesus, noticing especially his self-giving love on our behalf. The shadow of his cross has the power to bring all things to light. To be "holy" is to understand God *as in Christ*, and then allow that understanding to reshape who we are into whose we are, God's children re-imaged into the likeness of Jesus Christ.

Enriching Our Understanding

An Artful Balance. The heart of John Wesley's theology is an artful balance of *holiness* and *love*. Balanced is a complete otherness (God as holiness, fully set apart) and a graceful reaching for us (God as merciful love). The One who is like no other, and in need of nothing, nonetheless actively seeks to restore and have communion with us fallen creatures. Such a *holiness-love* combination guides in understanding the wonderful nature of God and thus the intended nature and possibility of the Christian life.

Holiness without love easily leads believers to isolation and indifference dominated by strict rules and cultural taboos. Many

Christians in the holiness tradition have faulted in this direction. If love dominates, largely separated from holiness, it easily becomes self-indulgent and gets lost in "spiritual narcissism."[5] But if holiness is combined with love in artful balance, as it is in God, one has an excellent understanding both of God's nature and of God's intention for Christian life. The various dimensions of such balance are explored in the following chapters.

God as Complex Dynamism. The revelation of God in the Old Testament "partakes exactly of the qualities of complexity, dynamism, and fluidity that belong to our post-modern world. A fresh perception of God as in the Old Testament goes a long way toward letting this God be a contemporary partner in a world that is open and in process. We must not be tempted to solve societal (and thus personal) problems by reducing solutions to power or technology or more commodity goods."[6] The solution lies in God with us and in us and for others. God is the dynamism of the three-in-one (Trinity) and the holy-love balance.

What Is Christian Holiness? "Holiness is nothing more than living full of the Master, Jesus, who is holy. It is the convening center that begins with the Master and extends outward in our lives. It creates healing and wholeness in a way that integrates who we are inside with what we do in our behavior. And who better to provide that center than God, whose very nature is holiness. God is the Master who is to become visible in us."[7]

The Enriched Ones. Christian holiness is being on the right pilgrimage through life, the one described in Psalm 84. How wonderfully rich are those who draw their inspiration and direction from God, whose very hearts are focused on God. They are the ones who wend their way through this fractured world functioning as springs

---

[5] This phrase and the "artful balance" are identified and explained in more detail in Kenneth J. Collins, *The Theology of John Wesley*, Introduction.

[6] Walter Brueggemann, *The Unsettling God.*

[7] Kevin Mannoia, *Masterful Living.*

of healing, reservoirs of life-giving power to the sick, the weak, and the empty lives that they touch about them.

Nothing truly good or worthwhile is kept from those who walk within the will of the holy God. They can sing these wonderful words as they travel: "Frail children of dust, and feeble as frail, in Thee do we trust, nor find Thee to fail."[8] To know the holy God is to sing in true wonder:

> Oh Lord, my God, when I, in awesome wonder,
> Consider all the worlds Thy hands have made;
> I see the stars, I hear the rolling thunder,
> Thy power throughout the universe displayed.
>
> Then sings my soul, my Savior God to Thee,
> How great Thou art, how great Thou art;
> Then sings my soul, my Savior God to Thee
> How great Thou art, how great Thou art.[9]

A Call to Action

We must go back to the experience of the prophet Isaiah, chapter 6. He glimpsed God "high and lofty," with the hem of the divine robe touching where the amazed and humbled prophet sat. Those in attendance around God were calling to each other, "Holy, holy, holy is the Lord of hosts; the whole earth is full of his glory!" Isaiah suddenly realized his complete unworthiness. But then he was touched by a cleansing coal and commissioned to be a new man, God's humble, holy representative in the world. Isaiah's response? "Here am I; send me!"

How will you know that you've caught a fresh vision of the holy God? It's when you gratefully bow in humility and begin adoring and worshipping God "not for what he has done for you or you expect him to do, but for what God has been from eternity before we existed, and for what God will be forever—it's that which captivates us and evokes from us the offering of self in worship."[10]

---

[8] Based on Psalm 104, composed by Robert Grant.

[9] Beloved song of praise by Carl Bolberg (1885).

[10] Albert E. Day, *An Autobiography of Prayer*, quoted by Bob and Michael Benson, *Disciplines for the Inner Life*.

Will you embrace this vision for yourself and allow these heavenly hymn words to arise from deep within? "Holy, holy, holy, Lord God Almighty!"[11]

---

[11] Words of the hymn *Holy, Holy, Holy* by Reginald Heber, based on Revelation 4:8.

What is Christian Holiness?

Paul captured the core truth. What really matters is that one become a genuinely *new creation* (Gal. 6:16). Beyond rules of holy behavior, it's our actual identity that needs radically changed. After real "conversion," a true turning around of life, one then is to be enabled to look with eyes other than their own and love with an intensity that comes only as a gift from the loving Father.

Earthrise

Earth, a little blue marble in the vastness of space. How fragile and insignificant it is, and now how spoiled. Still, it's the object of God's love, the fortunate focus of God's intent to re-create. By God's holy grace, the Earth is ready to rise! God is not satisfied with spoilage. The Holy One is at work on behalf of a renewed creation. "The power of the living God does not consist in God's keeping everything in absolute dependence. It's found in the fact that God 'bears' everything in endless patience, thereby creating a space for them and leaving time to develop in freedom."[1]

The Holy Creation Now Must be a Holy Re-creation.
Christian Holiness is . . . Accepting God's Re-creation.
Genesis 1; Galatians 2

---

[1] Jürgen Moltmann, *The Living God and the Fullness of Life*.

In 2018 the United States marked the 50th anniversary of the great sermon "I've Been to the Mountain" by Martin Luther King, Jr. That same year I keyed off this anniversary by co-editing *Views from the Mountain*, the lifetime writings of my dear brother, James Earl Massey, a friend of King and himself a wise prophet who died in 2018. That year saw all of this and more. The composition of possibly the most beloved of all Christmas songs, *Silent Night*, marked its 200th anniversary in 2018.

Silent Night, Troubled Planet. Some of the classic words of the beloved Christmas song are, "Silent night, holy night, All is calm, all is bright, Christ the Savior is born." I rejoice in the message of that birth, surely a pivotal point in divine revelation and human history. However, when that night actually happened, most people didn't receive warmly the holy child in that little town of Bethlehem, and most humans still are not following the way of life he graciously brought. On that silent night, few things were calm—and immediately after it seemed like all was going terribly wrong.

Not much has changed, unfortunately. All is hardly calm or especially bright these days of the third decade of the third millennium after that holy birth. We still need a new lightening flash to jolt our blindness and complacency. We still need another trip to the mountaintop of divine revelation, a fresh view to give perspective to the chaotic life on this little planet Earth. And yes, our globe is very little in the grand scheme of things.

The bigger the telescopes we build the more amazing appears the extensiveness of all that's out there. The psalmist is surely right: "When I consider Your heavens, the work of Your fingers, the moon and the stars which You have ordained, what is humanity that You take thought of it and care for it?" (Ps. 8:3-4).

The year 2018 marked yet another grand event. Fifty years earlier three humans had flown into orbit for the first time, circling the Moon ten times, and returning safely to the clutches of Earth's gravity. Even if only briefly, humans finally had escaped their home planet! The crew of Apollo 8, with the lunarscape as foreground, snapped an amazing photo on Christmas Eve, 1968. Now called

Earthrise, it dramatically shows the Earth in all its smallness and yet marbled and rounded beauty.

So Foolish We Are! How blue and pristine, and how terribly fragile is this bit of space debris on which we live. The Earth seems so lovely and lonely as it floats in the vastness of space. The 1968 picture by the first of our planet's space travelers was the first sight of ourselves in a mirror. Hundreds of millions of people in all nations were captivated by the sight of a slightly misshapen bowling ball rolling around in deep darkness, with all its inhabitants somehow hanging on to the surface they knew they were increasingly polluting.

This distant image of the Earth should have accomplished more than it did. It should have put an end to our petty human conceits and launched a fresh determination to care for this tiny pale blue treasure, our little home amidst the unknown vastness of dark and cold space. The reality, however, is now all too obvious. Earth is cosmically insignificant, and yet it's all we have as a human species. No national boundaries are visible in the photo. No hostilities between people groups can be seen or seem to make any sense. And yet, how real they are, how foolish we are!

We are together on this tiny celestial ship, sailing on unknown and apparently endless seas of space. We are so blessed and, by our choice, so endangered. We are so loved by the holy God and yet so stuck on ourselves. The humbling sight made the Apollo 8 astronauts want to come home and break down all national and cultural barriers troubling humans and their floating little world. They offered to the world a space-reading from the book of Genesis. How contemporary seemed those lines of the ancient creation story. How little we apparently understand about the immensity of the creation or the holy majesty and loving patience of the Creator.

Those astronauts might have gone on to sing the haunting lines of *Silent Night*. Looking from so far away, this planet, the humble home of us humans, is indeed bright and calm, at least when viewed from a great distance. It also is so in need of a Savior. Jesus came long ago, came from the distant heart of the Father that was wanting to be so near to us troubled and loved humans. In that Jesus event was embedded the comprehensive reality of God that extends beyond the limits of even our fondest imaginations.

God, so distant that he was before anything else, suddenly came close as a baby lying in an earthly feeding trough. That baby was bringing to a passing speck in the sky the hope of life which is eternal, which resonates with the stars, which extends beyond our or any universe and has no ending. It's the holy life that gracefully participates with God's own, a life that will endure long after the creation itself is no more. Merry Christmas!

Easter Amazement. Could it be, eternal life, the very life of God with and in us? Could it be, the Creator graciously re-creating in his image and in our own time? I have at least tasted that divine life and am forever grateful. My prayer is that the whole of humanity finally will come to realize and sing, "Joy to the world, *the Lord has come!*" Originally, God created everything from nothing. God now continues to create, this time from the scattered and spoiled pieces of the original creation. The Holy One works in love with the unholy to restore what it once was and again can be.

Unfortunately, all the evil that now is so unlike God resists any troubling of its status quo. The opponents of Jesus conspired to have him crucified, a brutal and disgraced dumping of a living being back to the dust, an apparent reversion of Jesus to the nothingness of earthly oblivion. Then came again the Creator's divine voice, hovering over troubled waters and saying, *"Let there be."* And there was!

It was the arrival again of order out of chaos, a releasing of light in darkness, the emergence of new life. It was resurrection, Jesus alive forevermore, a re-creative act of God bringing the hope of eternal life for the most undeserving of us. Holy God, holy action, an opportunity for holiness again.

Easter is an amazing possibility for all of fallen creation. Why? Because the holy God loves and hasn't given up on us. Jesus being raised from the dead was a cosmic event that reopened the future and now offers new life for us all, a holy life provided by a holy God. The very life of today's Christian church depends on the ongoing dynamism of the tomb of Jesus being shockingly empty. The future relies on the Spirit of Jesus continuing to hover over our troubled waters with loving and redeeming intent.

The Center of All Christian Theology. The central message of the New Testament is this. Since Jesus lives, we too can live, now, wonderfully, and always! Since God is, so can we be, not by our own doing or deserving but by the grace of the Holy One who created and chooses to create again out of love. Earth-rise, humanity-rise. How? Because is who God is and Jesus is risen indeed!

Why. did Jesus ever come, die, and rise in the first place? Why is Christian holiness so central in the Christian's vision of God and of our own potential as redeemed and restored humans? The answer lies in the correction of a widespread misunderstanding among so many contemporary Christians. They believe that honoring God surely must begin with stressing above all that God is *sovereign*, that God orders all the affairs of the creation by unilateral, irresistible decree. That leads to an election concept featuring the predestination of some to eternal life and some to a deserved eternal damnation.

In this attempt to honor God by insisting on ultimate and irresistible power, we inadvertently are led to a defective view of God, humans, sin and salvation. Although the sovereignty of God certainly is real, it's a secondary category when applied to God. Prior to the original creation, sovereignty couldn't have been a part of God's experience because there were no subjects to rule. "The primary category for God was established by the relationships within God's triune personhood, where his fatherhood existed prior to his sovereignty."[2]

God is, by eternal nature, a *love-infused, interactive relationality*. That's why the Trinity (Father, Son, Spirit) is so key a doctrine in the Christian faith. That's why Christian holiness is also so important in the Christian's vision of all reality--as it originally was, not largely isn't, and presently is God's intention to restore. "Sin" is a selfish violation of the God-creature relationship. "Holiness" is the restoration state of that original and yet intended divine-human relationship. God, love-infused by nature, chooses a costly interaction with

---

[2] Dennis Kinlaw, *The Mind of Christ*.

fallenness on behalf of restoring this proper relationship. Such love defines much of the meaning of sovereignty.

Exploring the Biblical Text

Genesis 1. The original creation was judged "very good" (Gen. 1:31). Soon it was ruined by human disobedience. Adam and Eve tried to be "like God" by doing as they pleased in defiance of divine intentions and instructions. God responded with judgment and forgiveness, and eventually even with coming sacrificially in the person of his Son, Jesus. In the face of human waywardness, the Creator seeks to recreate out of the abundance of divine love.

Yes, God's creating still goes on. Love hasn't given up. The present goal is for us sinners to be newly alive "in Christ," with original holiness restored. We again are given opportunity to reflect in our redeemed characters the loving nature of God. To be holy is to willingly be what God intends by the grace of God active in our lives.

Galatians 2. Our testimony can be that of Paul. "I have been crucified with Christ, and it is no longer I who live, but Christ who lives in me" (2:20). To be a true Christian "apostle" originally was thought to require having been with Jesus personally and witnessed his resurrection appearances. In fact, Paul met neither of these qualifications. However, he insisted that he was a true apostle because Jesus had chosen to meet him personally on the road to Damascus. We all can be new in Christ, apostles of the Master, only because God in Jesus comes to us personally on our worldly roads.

Paul had failed to gain favor from God by being Jewish and obeying the Law, but by having faith in Jesus the Christ. Abraham himself had gained God's favor by faith before there ever was the Law of the Jews. Salvation isn't dependent on what we do *for God* but on what God in Jesus has done *for us*. To be holy is to receive what we could never earn or create. It comes only in restored relationship with God as enabled by divine grace. Our prayer should be, in the classic words of Charles Wesley:

> Finish then Thy new creation,
> Pure and spotless let us be;
> Let us see Thy great salvation,
> Perfectly restored in Thee.

Enriching Our Understanding

God Loves the Created Order. The message of "perfect love" for God and neighbor *in this life* provides an optimism about the possibilities of grace in human existence, societies, and history, one that overcomes disabling despair. Christian holiness points to the validity and importance of human history. God cares about the now and the reality of our actual lives. We are to be God's representatives in this world and its troubled history, and we are to join God in the divine mission of redeeming and healing the creation.

The Genesis creation doctrine, including re-creation in the flood narrative, is a profound affirmation of God's predisposition to maintain an interactive and restorative relationship with this created order. It's as Jesus taught his disciples to pray: "May your reign arrive; may your will be done *on earth* as it is in heaven."[3]

Let's Be "In Christ"! Authentic Christian spirituality is personal life lived in union with Christ. It's a relationship with the incarnate and risen Lord through the power of the Holy Spirit. It's when the death of Jesus is my death, and his resurrection my resurrection. "Spirituality" in the New Testament sense is not a noble moral program, not merely a set of religious rules, not an advanced level of ethical achievement, not merely a philosophy or strategy for enhanced living. Instead, it's *life lived in Christ*.[4]

Co-Creators with God. When we believers go on mission, we are being asked by God to invest his re-creating resources for his glory. As God created us, we are to become co-creators with him as we work and play, live and die. Scripture suggests that this is God's intention. Paul calls on the children of God to deliver the creation

---

[3] See Michael E. Lodahl, in B. Callen and D. Thorsen, *Heart & Life*.
[4] See Barry L. Callen, *Authentic Spirituality*.

from the bondage of corruption into a glorious liberty (Rom. 8:19–21). God continues his creating, redeeming work, and asks us to be active agents of God in the process.[5]

A Call To Action

The Father of Jesus was the great Actor on both the original creation and more recent resurrection days. God creates and re-creates. You must see and count on this as you face what looks like a final grave. Jesus is the resurrection and the life, the once dying and now ever-living One. Being "holy" is to be like God, participating in his resurrection life and being an agent of his re-creating mission.

Can you sense such new-creation amazement coming over the horizon of your life? Recall that God "formed humans from the dust of the ground" and breathed life into their nostrils so that they became living beings (Gen. 2:7). Now you must become truly alive again by a new breathing of God's Spirit. You must begin functioning as a caretaker of God's beloved creation. Claim this privilege and accept this responsibility as your own. In other words, be holy as God is holy.

> Eternal God, whose power upholds
> both flower and flaming star,
> To whom there is no here nor there,
> no time, no near nor far,
> no alien race, no foreign shore,
> no child unsought, unknown;
> O send us forth, Thy prophets true,
> to make all lands Thine own![6]

---

[5] See Kevin Brown and Michael Wiese, *Work that Matters*.
[6] Lyrics by Henry H. Tweedy.

Providence or Politics?

Who or what really controls world events? If it's God, here's the only option. Since we don't get all the answers first, and then live confidently in their light, we humans must plunge into life by faith, being vulnerable and sometimes misunderstood, trusting the process, seeing only one step at a time. Jesus came to Nazareth. What did his hometown people see? A local kid showing off after abandoning a widowed mother and impoverished siblings. Can we see the truth when it's standing in front of us? So much goes on behind the scenes.

**The Holy Life is Guided by an Unseen Hand.
Holiness is . . . Embracing Invisible Guidance.
Psalms 85; Isaiah 30**

Awful things happen that we think wouldn't be allowed by a fully capable and loving God. Choices made by evil humans often are attributed to God can make little sense. If God is almighty and knows everything, is God in full control when things obviously violate his will? Why is there evil and why do good people suffer? These questions are real and never go away.

What also doesn't go away is the "mystery of Christ" now revealed by holy apostles and prophets through the Spirit of God (Eph. 3:4-5). The deepest of God's intentions usually are at work out of the sight. The full reality involves both foreground and background. Realizing that there is an eternal background is what gives meaning and hope to this strange and often chaotic life.

Says Paul, "We look not at what can be seen, but at what cannot be seen, for what can be seen is temporary, but what cannot be seen is eternal" (2 Cor. 4:18). We can at least glimpse by faith what for now is largely out of sight. It's God quietly at work. In Jesus, time and eternity were fused. He saw the whole of what was happening, foreground and background. "He alone belongs perfectly to both worlds."[1]

God is holy love. It's always active, whatever can or can't be seen or understood at present. Sanctified eyes begin to see, and find rest prior to full resolution of the evil. Being made alive in the Spirit, made holy, is the beginning of understanding spiritual matters that otherwise cannot be understood. It's "knowing the love of Christ that surpasses knowledge." It's receiving the riches of God's grace toward us in Christ Jesus that are "boundless" and "immeasurable." Such receiving yields unusual insight so that "we may be filled with all the fullness of God" (Eph. 3:19).

Know that God Will Provide. Humans generally see only what's on the surface and remember only what they choose to remember. How easily this subtle process of seeing so little and selecting our memories serve selfish ends. May God forgive our inability to perceive the depths of what is real and actually going on. Sin is blinding, concealing from our eyes the God who is very much at work, whatever the apparent circumstances.

---

[1] James S. Stewart, *Walking with God*.

The word that lies deep in the meaning of Christian holiness is "providence." It's derived from the word "provide" (Latin "forward" and "to see"). The English idiom "I'll see to it" shines light on the biblical meaning. God is saying to each humble believer, "I'll see to it in my time and way; relax, I'll provide." Whatever the circumstance at present, God promises an appropriate final result, and God is capable of ensuring that it indeed will be so.

The reported circumstance was critical. Where was the lamb for the offering? Abraham told his son, who nearly was the sacrifice, that "God will provide." A stray ram was spotted, Isaac was saved, and the place was called "The-Lord-Will-Provide" (Gen. 22:14). That's exactly the place where we can—must—live. Trusting in divine providence is the home of holy believers.

Holiness is being able to rest in God's assured promises, regardless of current circumstances. Wherever God looks, God acts for the good. God *sees* and eventually, somehow, *sees to it*. God's perception will come to include God's *provision*. God's holy children know this, rest in this, and make themselves available as instruments of its coming about as God may choose.

What has happened on the human scene that's so important and intentional on God's part that it should shape us rather than we shaping it? If the God of Abraham, Father of Jesus, and Lord of nations and creation, were to show us the real truth and focus our blurred memories on what's most important, what would we be seeing and remembering? This question should be our deepest human prayer.

Our human history, all those events, generations, battles and sufferings, joys and questions, have not been a random and empty process, the mere working of fate. What has been or will be has meaning because God, the ruler of nature and nations, has put a divine plot into the drama of history, making it truly *His-story*. It's the story of a good creation, a costly divine involvement addressing its evil, and eventually a glorious redemption. The foreground we know; this divine background we must come to know.

The holy ones of God lack answers to many things, but at least they can sing confidently about this being "our Father's world." Behind, beneath, and beyond everything is this. "The Lord Will Provide!" We are called to believe, and yet to be cautious. We must not cover harsh realities with glib little sayings, more shallow than helpful. For instance, it's of little help to say to someone in great pain, "Just relax, God's in full control." Or, "I know it makes no sense, but everything happens for a reason."

Holy disciples aren't to be full of platitudes, loaded with clever words that go beyond actual knowledge. However, we are granted knowledge of *Who* if not how, where, or when. Recall the prophetic words of Dietrich Bonhoeffer, executed by the Nazis. "Of course, not everything that happens is the will of God, yet in every event, however untoward, there always is a way through to God."[2] That's because the providence of God is always there, providing the way through.

What Has and Will Happen? When those ancient Israelites escaped their Egyptian bondage, it wasn't one of those numerous and annoying slave revolts. It wasn't even an escape. It was a *deliverance*. The Egyptians were baffled, the mountains trembled, and the sea had to get out of the way as the holy God chose and formed a people. Moses may have been up front, but God really was the leader. The Egyptians may have seen nothing divine about it, but that doesn't alter the larger reality. Surface observations may have concentrated on human determination and opportune events of nature. An adequate, a holy understanding, however, brings one back to the largely unseen providence of God.

Where is the wisdom in all the data of our "modern" days, the right perspective in the pluralistic maze that prevails in the twenty-first century? It always has been rooted in the presence and actions of God, usually behind the scenes, rarely acknowledged. There is within all things the stirring of love, the intent of redemption, the presence and coming provision of God. Behind the sound and fury of world events, somewhere in the shadows of time, stands the One who created the world and remains Lord over its events and Lover of its people.

God is anything but a cold, calculating manipulator. Nonetheless, God is the chief architect of time and eternity. In the final analysis, divine providence is more potent than human politics. Paul counsels

---

[2] Dietrich Bonhoeffer, *Letters and Papers from Prison*.

troubled believers in Corinth, insisting that there be no giving up just because things aren't what they should be. While on the outside it looks like everything is falling apart, on the inside God is making life new with his ever-unfolding grace (2 Cor. 4:13—5:1). There's so much more than meets the eye. The negatives obvious now are passing things. What's less obvious now is what soon will be clarified and last forever (4:18).

Here's an example that Paul holds before the Corinthians. The immediately obvious includes our frail bodies that grow older and weaker as the days go by. Momentary afflictions are real, but we who belong to Christ are not to focus on this passing reality. The larger fact is that our bodies, when folded like tents and stashed away, will be replaced by resurrection bodies that never will be put away again!

May we believers be "holy" by sensing the coming provision of God, standing on the divine promises instead of merely sitting on the church premises. May we be seeing by faith what God is doing now, although it's just out of sight. Let the mountains dance again! May the rivers that still obstruct and the captors who still enslave bow before the design that is deepest in things. When it happens, and "holiness people" know that it surely will, may all people finally come to recognize God's guiding hand and gladly join the holy ones in traveling in faith on the trail of divine destiny.

Exploring The Biblical Text

Psalm 85. Here we find a cascade of sung reminders of God's past faithfulness to the people of God. God is known best by knowing his past actions. He is remembered for having been gracious to the land, restored good fortune, forgiven iniquity, blotted out sins, withdrawn fury, and turned from wrath. The God of forgiving love, the Father of Jesus, has stood up to be known for who he really is and make clear what is expected of his children. "The Lord has shown us what is good, in Him are joined truth and grace; Before Him righteousness always goes, and His steps our pathway shows." Whatever we can't yet see, we must by faith see at least this. God is at work, even if behind the scenes. Eventually the background will resolve the foreground.

Isaiah 30. The prophet warns God's people that it's futile in the long-run to rely on Egypt for survival. The protection of Pharaoh would become their shame. Habakkuk agrees: "Woe to him who says to wood, 'Come to life!' or to a lifeless stone, 'Wake up!' It is covered with gold and silver, but there is no breath in it" (2:19). By contrast, "When you turn to the right or the left, your ears shall hear a word behind you, saying, 'This is the way, walk in it'" (30:21). God is guiding and will provide. Human alternatives always are abortive.

Isaiah warned Judah's King Ahaz to trust in God rather than relying for survival on worldly alliances. The sign given to Ahaz was the birth of a child (7:14). Before it would grow old enough to know the difference between good and evil, "the land before whose two kings you dread will be deserted." God is at work on our behalf behind the scenes. Public history is more than the balancing of brute power.

Matthew later would repeat this sign of the child, now in reference to the birth of Jesus (1:23). This time it was the dreaded Roman occupation, with the message to God's people the same. The baby's name shall be "Emmanuel" because indeed "*God is with us!*" His kingdom will be forever while the reign of all kings of the earth soon will be but dust under the chariot wheels of history. To be holy is to know this and dare to live accordingly.

Esther. Undoubtedly, a reason the book of Esther is included in Scripture is to show us the sovereign hand of God at work behind the scenes, caring for His people. While the name of God is never once mentioned, the observant reader is being shown God's hand in every circumstance, bringing about the deliverance of His people just as God had brought about their deliverance from Egypt. God was sovereignly at work through what appeared in the time of Esther to be especially evil circumstances. While God isn't mentioned, it's a big mistake to ignore him!

Enriching Our Understanding

God the "Almighty." "The truth of God's almightiness in creation, seen or unseen, is divine providence. It's the basis of all our trust, peace, and joy in God, the God of all our hopes of answered prayer, present protection, and final salvation."[3] Neither fate, nor the stars, nor blind chance, nor human folly, nor Satan's malice finally controls this world and its destiny. Instead, a morally perfect God is sovereignly in charge, and none can dethrone him or thwart his purposes of love. Holiness provides patience until the purposes of God's love become more apparent.

Focus on Love. The mystery of our faith is great" (1 Tim. 3:16). We believe in God who is unique, majestic, without limitations, whose providence is hardly comprehensible by mere humans. Questions are not fully answered and some Christian doctrines insist on being paradoxical.[4] To be confident of full knowledge is a sign of being deluded into a self-imposed idolatry. Fortunately, with the coming of Jesus, we are blessed with the ability to *apprehend* adequately what we cannot *comprehend* fully. God through Jesus Christ presents the proper angle of view. Especially in moments of suffering, wise believers focus on love and cease trying to explain what for now cannot be known.

God's Revealing Book. "I want to know one thing—the way to heaven; how to land safe on that happy shore. God Himself has condescended to teach the way: for this very end He came from heaven. He has written it down in a book. O give me that book! At any price, give me the book of God!"[5] The Bible's text is not an object over which we have control. We are to allow the text to become an instrument of God's grace in our lives. "The Bible stands close to the center of the whole process of being conformed to the image of Christ."[6] Holiness enables a learning from Scripture while

---

[3] J. I. Packer, as quoted by Stuart Briscoe, *The Apostles' Creed*.
[4] See Barry L. Callen, *Caught Between Truths*.
[5] John Wesley, Preface to *Sermons on Several Occasions*.
[6] M. Robert Mulholland, Jr., *Shaped by the Word*.

avoiding any attempt to "master" it. The Bible is God's sovereign voice reminding us of divine providence and calling us to trust it.

Remember, Then Forget. Remember God's great actions of yesterday, but don't allow looking back to block openness to seeing God acting in fresh and amazing ways today. Yesterday has wisdom to share. That wisdom, however, can sour if we get stuck back there and lose connection with today's fresh possibilities. "The faith memories of God's people help each new generation re-live God's past deeds of redemption, opening them to God's continuing activity in their own lives and times. Remembering is essential, although there must be no choking on mere nostalgia."[7] We believers are to be persons who remember with joy and then look forward expectantly, being certain of what we don't yet see (Heb. 11:1-12:3). To be holy is to remember well and look ahead with eyes peering behind the scenes for God's providence newly at work.

A Call To Action

God still is making history, not only by establishing a special people, but by ministering through this people on behalf of the good. To believe this and be transformed by this ultimate reality is hope and holiness.

> Lead on, O King eternal,
> the day of march has come,
> Henceforth in fields of conquest,
> Thy tents shall be our home.[8]

Look beyond today's headlines since so much good that's also going on isn't usually noticed or considered "news." Look at the night sky and know that what you see is but a tiny fraction of what's really there. Realize that the actions of those now in power, humanly speaking, won't be in charge for long. Do remember all those armies and invasions recorded in the Bible. Now forget them because they *all are gone*, but God remains present and active on behalf of your better future and that of all creation.

---

[7] Barry Callen and Steve Hoskins, *A Year with Rabbi Jesus* (vol. 1).
[8] Excerpt from the hymn "Lead On, O King Eternal" by Ernest Shurtleff.

God's future, while not yet fully realized, *will be!* "O God, our help in ages past, Our hope for years to come!"[9] We don't know many things, but this we can know. In all things, yes all, "God works for the good of those who love him" (Rom. 8:28-39). If God is for us, who can be against us? Only those whose futures already are doomed!

---

[9] The words of Isaac Watts, reflecting Psalm 90.

Who is Holy?

Who's a "saint" in God's eyes? It's someone who has become an extension of God's *hesed* (loving faithfulness). By God's grace, Christian saints are members of the covenant community of Christ, believers who are experiencing God's relational restoration and loving care, those who have gratefully become active in passing on to others this opportunity to belong and experience joy.

Let's Get Energized!

When if ever are we Christians "perfect"? If not perfection as usually conceived, can there at least be dramatic spiritual results of the ongoing "holiness" quest? Better descriptive words might be "focused" or "matured." I choose to think of believers being spiritually "energized," activated, really choosing to be on mission as intended. In what sense dare we Christians think of being privileged to "partake of God's nature"? The Bible insists that such is a real possibility if properly understood. Because God is reaching for restored communion with us, what can we be? We can be turned on to love! Beyond frail attempts at description is the reality of the turned-on experience.

Holiness is Partaking of God's Nature. Christian Holiness is . . . Being energized by God's Spirit.
2 Peter 1:3-5; Isaiah 57:15

One fact makes all else possible. There needs to be "an expectant faith rooted in an optimism of God's grace, an expanded vision of what God has promised in this present age, coupled with an intense longing to receive it."[1] Such vision and longing characterize a Christian holiness that actively seeks God's will being done on earth as in heaven. It's absorbing the Spirit's energy that awakens one from the spiritual stupor of the casual believer. It's "going on to perfection" in the sense of desiring all that Christ desires for us and through us as examples and agents of the kingdom of God on earth.

Going on spiritually involves an energizing of the ordinary Christian life, a new depth of spiritual breathing and acting. This coming awake centers in a conscious *letting go* of self-orientation, exhaling the old self, and a *letting God*, inhaling the new God-oriented self. Holiness is the journey from spiritual suffocation to a breath-full salvation that's energized inwardly with God's very life.

Holiness is a great motivator for Christian mission. Denominations emphasizing holiness have been especially active in movements on behalf of anti-slavery, women's rights, prohibition of social evils, and world mission. One denominational leader explains the "natural link" between the "deeper life" and worldwide evangelism. Receiving the power for holy living tends to enflame the desire for effective Christian witness.[2]

Awareness of this link is a Christian and not merely a Protestant thing. Pope John Paul II, in his encyclical *Redemptoris Missio*, wrote: "The call to mission derives, of its nature, from the call to holiness. A missionary is really such only if he commits himself to the way of holiness. The universal call to holiness is closely linked to the universal call to mission. Every member of the faithful is called to holiness and to mission. The church's missionary spirituality is a journey toward holiness."

Sharing God's Very Life. God has provided everything necessary for a full life of godliness. We are invited to become "par-

---

[1] Henry H. Knight, III, *Anticipating Heaven Below*. Also see Cliff Sanders, *The Optimism of Grace*.

[2] Bernie A. Van De Walle, *The Christian & Missionary Alliance*, in Barry Callen, ed., *The Holy River of God*.

ticipants of the divine nature" (2 Peter 1:4). Christian holiness is faith with excellence, a going on, a moving upward, possible only because God has come down to us in Jesus and now remains in his Spirit to make our rising possible.

Like water rolling and wind whipping the waves along, God moves in creative power. In the New Testament water is the medium in which a new believer is immersed in baptism, symbolizing entrance into new life because of God's gracious washing. Water is power and wind active in the person of God's Spirit, who breathes out God's very energy and new worlds emerge.

Christian holiness may be thought of as catching and being propelled by God's breath, the wind of the Spirit, and energized by God's life. Death is exhaled and the Spirit, God's life-giving presence and breath, is inhaled deeply so that we become Spirit people on the move in the Spirit's direction. Holiness always is far less something *achieved* by us believers and much more Someone *received.*

According to the Orthodox Christian tradition, we Christians are to adore God and receive "an influx of the divine." That is, we can be actual partakers of the divine nature, made holy by divine grace and because of the Spirit's active presence. We may be mere humans, always imperfect in several ways; nonetheless, we can *share* in the life of Christ, *receive* the healing and empowering of divine energy, and *reflect* God's loving nature in our living.

Propelled by Divine Energy. Understanding the phrase "divine energy" is crucial. There is a critical distinction between the *essence* and the *energies* of God. The very being of God (essence) is never ours. What we can receive by God's grace is the life (energies) of God so that we become God-like, although never God! Being "holy" by God's grace does not violate these beloved words of the hymn "Holy, Holy, Holy": "Only Thou art holy, There is none beside Thee, Perfect in power, in love and purity."

Only God is God, of course. Even so, God is both *high* and *nigh,* above, beyond, holy other, and also lovingly tender and always present and sharing. The prophet Isaiah speaks of God dwelling in the holy place, very different from where we dwell, and also choosing to be with us, right where we are (57:15), allowing us to participate in his energizing presence. The good news is that God will help us *participate* in the *energies* of his loving, holy nature. Our basic role as needy believers is to *let go* and *let God*. In that way, we become God-like in our life orientations and motivations.

Holiness is admittedly paradoxical, counter-cultural, a major reversal of the ordinary. It's a *falling upward*. The descent of God in Christ to our human scene happened so that we sinful humans might rise to a reuniting relationship with God through Christ. We can come to love because God first loved us. We can "go on to perfection" not because we are or will be "perfect" in ourselves and in this life. We go on because the Perfect One shares with us, infuses us, renews and sends us energized by his own life.

We go gracefully upward in the spiritual journey because the perfections of God come close and propel upward. As God's children, we naturally want to share characteristics of the Father. We are transformed into the likeness of Christ in order that we might be to others agents of God's glory and healing power shared with us.

Back in the Garden. When are we Christians "perfect"? When we are fulfilling the purpose for which we were created. God's original purpose was a world of relaxed, beautiful, self-giving, interactive love and lovers, as when God walked in joy with Adam and Eve in the garden, unhindered by sin. Babies can be "perfect," that is, wonderfully what they are meant to be at that stage of life, despite their immaturity and lack of knowledge. By God's restoring grace, we again can be garden-walkers with God. We can be freed of sin's domination, becoming all God intends and enables by the sharing of his "energies."

The holy ones are "adult" Christian believers, not measuring holiness by years old or time in the faith or level of gifting or volume of achievement. Spiritual growth continues before and after the experience of "Christian perfection." Even so, there comes a point in the faith journey when the love of God and neighbor begins to rule our "tempers, words, and actions."[3] That's when divine love has both *entered* and begun to *control* our lives of faith. That's when we

---

[3] John Wesley, in "Brief Thoughts on Christian Perfection" (1767).

are "holy," that is, wholly other than what we were and now truly for others in loving mission with Christ.

Many Christians spend too much time speculating about when Jesus will come again. They miss something of fundamental importance that enables holy lives in the meantime. At Pentecost, *Jesus came again!* The Spirit of Christ already has come *to us* to be *in us* (experienced holiness). Why? So that the Spirit can move *through us* as ministering love to a broken world (expressed holiness).[4]

Exploring the Biblical Text

Philippians 3:7-11. Christian holiness involves a believer's depth of desire to be like Christ. Psalm 1 speaks of "delight" in the Lord's law, while Psalm 63 calls for "earnestly" seeking God because the love of God is understood to be better than life itself. Peter says we are to crave God's goodness as a baby desires milk when really hungry (1 Pet. 2:1–10). Paul considers everything loss compared to the surpassing greatness of knowing Christ Jesus our Lord. Oh, how we should want to know Christ and the power of his resurrection! Christian holiness is faith with intensity, love with delight, a craving after the goodness of God that surpasses all else.

2 Peter 1:3-5. "God's divine power has given us everything needed for life and godliness, through the knowledge of him who called us by his own glory and excellence. He has given us his precious and very great promises, so that through them we may escape from the corruption that is in the world because of lust and may become participants of the divine nature. For this very reason, we must make every effort to support our faith with excellence."

Believers seeking holiness must add to faith knowledge of ourselves as known by God, of God as revealed in Jesus Christ, and of what we are being enabled to become in light of Christ. As the "fruit of the Spirit" grow within (Gal. 5:22–24), the humbled believer thinks and acts increasingly in holy, Christ-like ways, not because "I must" but because "I *want!*"

---

[4] Barry L. Callen, *Catch Your Breath!*

> More like Christ my heart is praying,
> More like Christ from day to day;
> All his graces rich displaying,
> While I tread my pilgrim way.[5]

Enriching Our Understanding

Holiness Is Beautiful Joy! Christians need to rediscover the beauty of holiness by being painted personally with the brilliant, splendorous, glorious, delightful, restorative colors of God. Only then will we know the sheer joy of having such grace poured on us like rain on a dry and thirsty land. It was this and only this that could cause the early disciples of Jesus to "consider it all joy" when they encountered various trials (Jam. 1:2). They could embrace suffering as a kind of glory (Phil. 3:10) and even sing in the darkness (Acts 16:25). *Joy to the World* should be more than a popular Christmas carol. It's the Christian's theme song![6]

"Perfection" in Every Stage of Growth. The command for the Christian to be spiritually "perfect" is unfortunate because this word is now so misleading. John Wesley's classic book *A Plain Account of Christian Perfection* uses many of its pages to clarify what is *not* meant. Perfection, however, does apply in various ways to a child of God in various stages of spiritual experience. "A blade of corn may be said to be perfect in a dozen different stages of its growth. But if, before it's ripe, it stops growing, it then would not be perfect. So, at a certain period of spiritual experience, a person may be said to be a 'perfect' Christian, even if spiritual attainments are small in comparison with what they yet will be."[7]

God Energizes Men and Women Equally. "Wesleyan/Holiness women since John Wesley's time have testified to the fact that, for them, empowerment for leadership accompanied the experience of holiness. Their resulting ministries demonstrated the power of the

---

[5] Charles Wesley Naylor, "More Like Christ."
[6] Hubert P. Harriman and Barry L. Callen, *Color Me Holy*.
[7] B. T. Roberts, *Editorial Writings of the late Rev. Benjamin T. Roberts, A. M.*

Holy Spirit in their lives. They effectively challenged the ethic of domesticity which sought to confine them within the walls of their homes. Armed and energized with the gift of divine power, women overcame the 'man-fearing spirit' and moved outside their homes, refusing to limit their ministries to their immediate families."[8]

A theology of empowerment has enabled women to fulfill their own callings from God. Holiness is empowerment regardless of gender. It also provides a courageous energy for confronting evil. Within the current family network of the *Wesleyan Holiness Connection* is the "Junia Project," an online community of women and men advocating for the inclusion of women in church leadership. Also affiliated is the *Wesleyan Holiness Women Clergy* organization that provides support and resources to women called to ministry at every level of church life.[9] Holiness as a Christian experience leans toward gift-based rather than gender-based or race-based ways of defining appropriate ministers and ministries.

A Call To Action

The biblical challenge is that we make every effort to support our faith with excellence. Everything needed is at hand by God's grace. Will you determine to move on spiritually, upward, closer to God's full will and provision for you? Allow yourself to become a "partaker of God's nature" and thus be an *energized participant* in God's mission today. To do so is to receive the Christ life in its fullness and be motivated to share that life with others hungering for help and hope.

Are you prepared to yield from self-centeredness to Christlikeness? Will you allow an inward flowing of the wind of God that will energize and send you passionately on God's loving mission? Since this is God's intention for you, it's a real possibility! Are you deserving? No! Even so, God's amazing love abounds and makes possible the impossible for us undeserving and yet intensely grateful believers.

---

[8] Susie C. Stanley, in Barry Callen and Don Thorsen, *Heart & Life*.

[9] See these and other current efforts at expressed holiness in Barry Callen, ed., *The Holy River of God*.

> On such love, my soul still ponder,
> Love so great, so rich, so free;
> Say, while lost in holy wonder,
> Why, O Lord, such love to me?[10]

The "why" of such wonderful love is the sheer grace of God. Note these words of one of the great holiness leaders of the nineteenth century:

> I see the new creation rise,
> I hear the speaking blood;
> It speaks, polluted nature dies,
> Sinks 'neath the cleansing flood.
>
> I rise to walk in Heav'n's own light,
> Above the world and sin,
> With heart made pure and garments white,
> And Christ enthroned within.[11]

---

[10] From the lyrics of "Sovereign Grace O'er Sin Abounding" by John Kent.
[11] From the lyrics of "The Cleansing Wave" by Phoebe W. Palmer.

Travel the Whole Salvation Road

The Christian spiritual life is a journey and not just one or two intense emotional experiences. Being "justified," forgiven, is basic and amazing, but freedom from past sin isn't enough. Believers must then seek the higher spiritual road, "sanctification," the holy road, the "more excellent way." It includes not being so intoxicated by God's wondrous love that we become paralyzed by paradise. There can be no praise orientation that makes us action anemic. To be holy is to be about God's business. Get ready to move on up and travel on down the salvation road. The Christian life is more than arriving one day in heaven. It's about activating heaven here and now.

Holiness is God's Intent for Us All. Don't Stop Short. Christian Holiness is . . . Traveling the Pilgrim's Faith Road. Colossians 1:8-11; 1 Corinthians 12:27-31

"Pilgrim" is an apt word for the Christian journey. It began with Abraham launching into the dark unknown in faith and later Israel wandering in the wilderness in search of the promised land. Paul continues this image by praying for endurance and patience as believers in Jesus keep walking and growing in their knowledge of God (Col. 1:10). My own autobiography is titled *A Pilgrim's Progress*. Since it's now in its fourth edition, apparently there's a long way to go and no place to stop.

Unfortunately, many Christian believers have never considered or have abandoned the quest for the highest calling of God on their lives. They are forgiven of yesterday's sin but not divinely indwelt and controlled and actively serving. They know Jesus as Savior but never have yielded their lives to him *as Lord*, not going far enough down salvation's road to be caught up in becoming active agents of the divine purpose. Taking the lordship of Christ seriously must come to mean that all of life has been yielded to divine control and focused on the divine mission.

Christian holiness is such yielding and focusing. Beyond the courtroom scene of sin being pronounced forgiven is the cemetery scene, being *resurrected*, shedding the old self and being clothed with a new self, the Christ-self. God desires to do more after the salvation trial than issue new identity cards so we can be called "Christians." God graciously wishes to create new spiritual life so that we can come to live *into* and *out from* actual new life in Christ. We need to be both forgiven and resurrected, bills paid and life itself refashioned and sent on a new mission.

Becoming Resurrection People. Disciples of Jesus must deal with the crowds of this world. The crowd usually sets the pace, defines the terms, and shows the currently acceptable and thus the easy way to go. It provides enticements and distractions to the way of Jesus. Will life be one of love, forfeiting personal ego and ambition in favor of faithfulness to the Master in the face of the crowds? Such eternal life involves a personal dying, something that leads to real living. It's the Cross-Resurrection pattern of giving up the selfish and sinful life in favor of the well-being of others.

Paul puts it clearly to the Ephesians: "You were dead" (2:1) but now you are "alive together with Christ" (2:5). God raised Jesus from the dead (1: 20); he also "raised us up with him" (2:6). A dramatic resurrection launched the ongoing life of Jesus. Resurrection now can launch ours as well, in this life, not only after death. We were sin-dead. Now God is prepared to make us *resurrection-alive*. Beyond a sin record that's cleared in God's eyes is to come a new heart that beats with Christ's, new blood that flows from God's throne, and a new will that is one with God's own love.

While resurrection may happen all at once, it takes time to absorb its full reality and engage its many implications. We who have been sinners for years tend to carry old cemetery habits and assumptions into this new resurrection country of holiness. Therefore, we new "saints" require patience as we are reorientated into the resurrection conditions that are to prevail. By God's grace and over time, we can and will find our way of *living into* and then actually *living out of* the new resurrection world, being reflective of the "full stature of Christ" (Eph. 4:13).

Slow Traffic on the Road. The "holy ones" among Christian believers are not the bragging spiritual elites, the celebrated champions of the faith, the brightly shining "stars" among the Jesus people. Instead, more likely they are the most humble and selfless. They are the stabilizers in the church who have this testimony: "I'm pressing on the upward way, new heights I'm gaining every day, still praying as I'm onward bound, Lord, plant my feet *on higher ground*."[1]

Christians too often settle for walking a lower spiritual path. Forgiven of past sin, they become spiritually satisfied and remain immature in their faith journey. Without having to carry around a burden of guilt, they become spiritually passive. They are evangelized but not discipled, born anew but stunted in growth, belonging to Christ but not evidencing a dramatic inward change. Going through the motions of respectable religion may be satisfying at a certain level, but it's certainly not enough. The prophet Amos who cried out against Israel for their settling for far less than intended, disappointing and finally disgusting God.

---

[1] Johnson Oatman, Jr., *Higher Ground* (1898).

The way of Christ intends to raise the eyes of faith upward, to encourage a noticing of the bright orange that is breaking over the horizon. It's a call John Wesley once explained. "Whoever finds redemption in the blood of Jesus has then the choice of walking in the higher or the lower path. I believe the Holy Spirit at that time sets before the believer the 'more excellent way,' inspiring a seeking after the heights and depths of holiness, after the entire image of God."[2]

We Jesus people are called to travel the whole salvation road. Being "saved" must come to include learning who we should be apart from sin's guilt and then domination. It's becoming "holy" in this very world. It's to be "sanctified," set apart and made new in Christ by the Holy Spirit. We are to be saved both *from* sin and its consequences and then *for* God's ongoing mission.

> Open my mouth, and let me bear,
> gladly the warm truth ev'rywhere;
> Open my heart and let me prepare
> love with Thy children thus to share.
> Silently now I wait for Thee,
> Ready my God, Thy will to see,
> Open my heart, illumine me,
> Spirit divine![3]

These lines, based on Psalm 119, seek the fuller, the more excellent way, being properly grounded spiritually and then activated by the Spirit through divine gifts designed for service.

Understanding the meaning of "sin" is vital. The Bible views sin as a *relational* breakdown. God loves and the human who chooses to violate that love relationship has sinned. It's the choice to eat forbidden fruit by refusing obedience to God's will. The "entire" of entire sanctification refers to the wholeness of the renewed relationship between a humbled heart and the healing God. There must be immediacy and intimacy in the renewed relationship with Christ that take one out of oneself and into the world on mission with Christ.

---

[2] John Wesley in his sermon "The More Excellent Way."
[3] Clara Scott, *"Open My Eyes, That I May See."*

Let Go, Let God, and Move On! The first act of sin-healing is conversion, turning around and getting pointed in the God-ward direction. The new child of God then must go on to the experience of the fullness of what that initial blessing promises. The second act of sin-healing involves a divine addressing of the ongoing power of sin. We Christians do more than commit sin, requiring forgiveness. We also are infected by the sin disease, requiring a change of our very characters.

Once turned from the sins of the past, there comes a lifelong spiritual journey of gaining a new Christ-like being for the future. There remains beyond forgiveness a "weight" problem. We are called to "lay aside every weight, and the sin that clings so closely" (Heb. 12:1). Christians living this "more excellent way" have shed the heavy weight of the old life, exhaling death and assuming the lightness of inhaling the life of the Spirit of God. It's an in-depth moving of the "me" from the throne of life so that Christ comes to live and control within (Gal. 2:20). Shedding the weight of sin centers in *letting go* and joyously *letting God*.

There is God's "most excellent way" (1 Cor. 12:31). The holy God always has holiness in mind for us fallen and forgiven human beings. Getting on the salvation road is one thing; actively traveling that road is another. "Holiness is moving down the road by being truly re-born, re-formed, and re-engaged, a comprehensive re-relating to the holy God in ways that begin to show clearly in how we think and value and act."[4]

Like in a dramatic production, there are first-act and second-act disciples of Jesus. Group one includes the believers who have limited themselves to getting their sinful pasts forgiven. Group two includes those who are forgiven and actively going on to allow Jesus to reshape them into holy and serving representatives of God, even in the most difficult of circumstances. The first group, we sometimes say, are being "saved" and the second also "sanctified." That is, the second are becoming real disciples in the image of and on the mission of the Master.

"Lightning still flashes around the throne of God. Its bright colors and electric power, its gentle shades and loving kindness, its roll-

---

[4] Barry L. Callen, *Catch Your Breath!*

ing thunder and overwhelming presence combine to give us at least a glimpse of the true God. The Holy One, quite apart from us, nonetheless reaches our way in holy love as the Great Artist who wishes to *color us holy*."[5] Being forgiven? Yes. Changing life colors? YES! We must begin and then go on.

Exploring The Biblical Text

Romans 5 and 6. *Loving* is the key that must be associated with *living*. Sins forgiven is the important beginning of the Christian meaning of "salvation," but only the beginning. Forgiveness must go on to involve transformation. The promise of "justification" in Romans 5 is followed by the call to "union," to "sanctification" in Romans 6. If there is no newness of life, no union with Christ, no coming out from under the dominion of sin, no yielding to the wooing of God's Spirit to come home to life in God's love, there's not the *fullness* of salvation that God intends.

Colossians 1:8-11. Paul learned that the congregation in Colossae was filled with love in God's Spirit. He prayed that they would move on and gain even more fullness of the knowledge of God's will. Why? It was in order that they might "walk worthy of the Lord, fully pleasing to him." To deal with the troubles being faced, they needed to grow in the wisdom that yields "endurance and patience." The more one walks the holy way the more one understands and is anxious to travel on. Knowing God ignites the flame of wanting to know God more and more. Engaging the world in God's name requires a richer relating to God that in turn illumines the way one is to go.

1 Corinthians 12:27-31. Believers in Jesus comprise the church of Christ. Church leaders are called by God and gifted in various ways for their divinely appointed roles. Christian holiness is functioning within the body as members not jealous of each other's callings and giftings but "striving for the greater gifts, the "more excellent way." That way allows God to gift and guide the church

---

[5] Hubert P. Harriman and Barry L. Callen, *Color Me Holy*.

as he chooses. It provides the proper context of prevailing love that enables unity in the midst of diversity (chap. 13). A divided and contentious church may know forgiveness of past sin but isn't yet far enough down the salvation road. It must determine to experience the corporate holiness essential for successfully engaging together the intended mission of the church.

Enriching Our Understanding

Almost to Altogether. "May we all thus experience what it is to be not *almost* but *altogether* Christians! May we be justified freely by God's grace, through the redemption that is in Jesus, knowing we have peace with God, being able to rejoice in hope of the glory of God, and having the love of God shed abroad in our hearts by the Holy Ghost given unto us!"[6] "Altogether" is to have journeyed on down the salvation road.

A Loving Relationship with Jesus. "I am called to be absolutely Christ-like. This is a monumental claim upon my life. The perfection to which I am called certainly does not mean that I will ever be free from ignorance or mistakes or infirmities or temptations. Rather, God calls me to develop such a close and loving relationship with Jesus that I would never want to do anything to separate myself from that love or withhold it from anyone else."[7] Being holy is to be in a restored relationship with God through Christ by the Spirit that is so intimate and love infused that one determines never to "sin," that is, to consciously violate the known will of God.

A Willing Commitment of the Self. "To be truly 'sanctified' demands moral decision. We must come to the crisis of self-abandonment to the will of God after we have become painfully aware of our remaining self-centeredness and double-mindedness. Consecration moves on a deeper level than the initial surrender to Christ for pardon. Its motivation is a deepened conviction of the pervasive nature of the self-will. It's the frank and contrite acknowledgment

---

[6] John Wesley, "The Almost Christian."

[7] Paul Chilcote, *Praying in the Wesleyan Spirit*.

of one's pettiness, ambition, pride, and selfishness, and a conscious, willing commitment of the self in love to God."[8] The sanctifying journey of Christian holiness is seen in the four final lines of the verses of a great hymn:

> "All of self, and *none* of Thee!"
> "*Some* of self, and *some* of Thee!"
> "Less of self, and *more* of Thee!"
> "*None* of self, and *all* of Thee!"[9]

A Call To Action

Who is a Christian, a *whole* Christian, a *holy* Christian? It's the grateful person "knowing Father and Son and walking along the pathway of cross and resurrection through the power of the Spirit. We must be personally crucified and buried with Christ and then risen with Christ in new life in the Spirit."[10] Is a holy wholeness yet your spiritual goal? If not, are you ready to let it be? The health of the church and the success of its mission depend in part on your seeking the more excellent way.

In his sermon "The Wedding Garment," John Wesley makes plain that "orthodoxy" is only a part of religion and must not be mistaken for the substance of the faith—which is *holy love reigning in the heart*. Is your heart yearning for the brightest light coming from Christ for you? "Let Thine image in me appear, Light of holiness bright and clear, Light of faithfulness, free from fear, Shine, O shine in me."[11]

---

[8] William Greathouse, *Love Made Perfect*.

[9] Words by Theodore Monod, quoted by James Stewart in *The Gates of New Life*.

[10] Clark H. Pinnock, *Flame of Love*.

[11] Words by Charles Wesley Naylor. See 2 Corinthians 3:18.

Watch Your Language

Christians are to live and share a holy "Yes!" God's promises are positive for those living by the Spirit of Jesus. Claiming and then living them is essential for our Christian testimony to others. Displaying and verbalizing a positive and hopeful attitude regardless of circumstance is the social media of the Spirit. Speaking the "YES!" properly is necessary to avoid spoiling the witness to what is so good. God gives new speech. Believers are to master that speech, ever guarding their tongues. In addition to holy hearts and sanctified hands, we are to be careful communicators so that our mouths share authentic messages of Christ being truly in us on behalf of others.

Holiness Involves the Inspired Speech of God
Christian Holiness is . . . Communicating a "YES" to Life. 2 Timothy 4:16-18; James 1:19-26

Praing, living, and communicating positively "in the Spirit" is a holy task (Eph. 6:18). Jude 20 instructs: "But you, dear friends, build yourselves up in your most holy faith and pray in the Holy Spirit." There are times when our normal speech fails us and God's Spirit must assist in our addressing the Father in thoughts deeper than our feeble words can manage. We must watch our language. The Lord taught us what to seek in prayer. It centers in humble and holy attitudes and desires.[1]

New Testament writers often conclude prayers with "*Amen.*" Like the *shalom* of the Hebrew Bible, this word has a core meaning and a series of surrounding nuanced meanings. We can be confident that, when biblical people ended a serious conversation with God by saying "amen," they meant more than, "That's done. Time to move on to something else." The word was the heart of a human beating in tune with the heart of God. It was a public testimony to the beauty and truth and new-life possibilities in the prayer itself.

Really Mean "Amen!" Many biblical statements and prayers end with flourishes of joy and thanksgiving. One can sense the burst of holy meaning conveyed in the ending of Paul's second letter to Timothy: "The Lord will rescue me from every evil attack and save me for his heavenly kingdom. To him be the glory forever and ever. *Amen!*" (2 Tim. 4:18). We can almost feel the "Wonderful!" and "Yes!" in this "Amen!"

Despite our human unworthiness, God has spoken so well to us. God has said clearly in Jesus Christ a resounding "Yes!" Christian life, therefore, should be the pursuit of experienced and actually lived holiness, the amazing positives of the reign of God coming from Christ to us, and now in our speech through us to others. The church of Jesus should be the gathering of the "saints" for group exercises in speech development, skill in witnessing and evangelizing. Paul told the Corinthians that "all the promises of God in Jesus are Yes, and in him Amen, to the glory of God *through us*" (2 Cor. 1:20). God's amazing speech to us must be translated into our speech to others.

---

[1] Barry L. Callen, *The Prayer of Holiness-Hungry People: A Disciple's Guide to the Lord's Prayer.*

When completing the Lord's Prayer with a sincere "Amen!" we begin the disciple's path to perfection, not perfection of life performance, of course, but of complete commitment to the One through whom we now live and to whom belongs all glory, forever and ever. This "Yes!" should echo deep within us and radiate out from us. When we have prayed as directed by the One who himself carries the title "Amen," we echo the Bible's final book: "These are the words of the *Amen*, the faithful and true witness, the ruler of God's creation" (Rev. 3:14). We are to be speech-makers for God to the world. Let's get the scripts right and the tongues trained.

We disciples need to be careful with our language, not overstating the facts, and surely not claiming for ourselves any "perfection" which isn't the case—hypocrisy is hidden from very few. When we speak of Jesus, however, we should come up with language grand enough to cover the full reality. When speaking of him, we can let our language fly freely.

> Veiled in flesh the Godhead see,
> Hail the incarnate Deity,
> Pleased with us in flesh to dwell,
> Jesus, our Emmanuel.
> Hark, the Herald Angels sing,
> Glory to the newborn King![2]

Watch Your Words Carefully. Christian holiness is responding to God with our grateful "YES!" and committing to live in that wonderful wave of positive gratitude. Since in Jesus all the promises of God are "Yes!", we should "roll up our sleeves, put our minds in gear, and be totally ready to receive the gift. Don't leisurely slip back into those old grooves of evil. You didn't know any better then; you do now. As obedient children, let yourselves be pulled into a way of life shaped by God's life, a life energetic and blazing with holiness" (1 Pet. 1:13-16).

While being careful about language, and yet extravagant with it when appropriate, we Christian believers naturally shy from attaching the word "saint" to ourselves. Unfortunately, this word usually is reserved for highly accomplished Christians honored for their

---

[2] Charles Wesley, "Hark, How All the Welkin Rings."

outstanding spiritual specialness. In Ephesians and elsewhere, however, Paul doesn't hesitate to refer to *all* true believers as saints.

How can Paul justify this? He does it by emphasizing what God has done *for us*, not what we have accomplished *for him*. It's not how we feel about ourselves but how God feels about us.[3] Spiritual standing before God is less what we've *done* in our weakness and more what we've gratefully *received* from the strong hand of a loving God. We speak not about our level of spiritual maturity but about the lavish resources of a gracious God. To be a properly vocal, a Christian "saint" is not someone bragging on oneself but unleashing the highest of vocabulary about the God who exceeds whatever superlatives we can muster.

As a young man I was spiritually nourished by a woman pastor whom I would not hesitate to call a Christian saint. In interviewing her for the biography I wrote in gratitude, I inquired about why in all her sermonizing she never used personal illustrations. She answered, "Because I am so little and my Lord is so great that I haven't yet exhausted my speaking about him!"[4] Believers who focus on themselves eventually fall under divine judgment. The prophet Amos unleashes a series of bitter words that condemn self-centeredness (8:1-12), featuring of all things a fruit basket.

Who doesn't love a juicy bite of freshly picked fruit? The fruit basket of Amos, however, is horrifying. It leads immediately to talk of wailing and corpses. Why is fruit connected with death? The Hebrew word for "summer fruit" (*qayits*) is remarkably similar to the word for "end" (*qets*). This end word frequently carries deadly overtones (Gen. 6:13; Lam. 4:18; Ezek. 7:2–3). Amos clearly had been called to announce the coming of severe judgment of the religiously self-indulgent who shared all the right words but had lost their meaning.

We must be very careful about the impact of our words on others. The typical message from God is conveyed best in love language. That's the best tongue for us believers to master and use regularly.

---

[3] This liberating truth is elaborated in Eugene Peterson's *Practice Resurrection*.

[4] See Barry Callen, *She Came Preaching* (Lillie S. McCutcheon).

Judgmentalism should be left to the rare prophet occasionally called by God for such a harsh purpose.

Church as a School of Language Development. Does "perfect love" reigning in the heart mean that the believer lives *entirely apart from sin*? The answer is "no" *if* what's meant by sin is anything that goes against God's perfect will, including sins of omission. If, however, we apply John Wesley's narrower definition of sin, "a willful transgression of a known law of God," then we may say that such a sinful pattern of behavior can be broken. The church should be a place for the breaking to happen.

The love of God can so fill the heart of the person who is wholly devoted to God that such love excludes sin. The love of God is purifying and freeing and empowering. Willful, rebellious disobedience is foreign to such love. Committing sin is never impossible, of course, but it would go against the very nature that can be developed in us by God's cleansing and empowering grace. Development, however, is necessary.

The love-purifying of our hearts ("sanctification") must be nurtured and maintained through the assistance of the community of faith. We must not forget the significance of the classes and bands instituted by John Wesley as critical support structures of the faithful. They assisted with the confessing of our faults one to another, praying for one another in order that all may be healed. Communal accountability and spiritual assistance are crucial.[5] It's language being refined for personal growth and public witness. Christian holiness is social in nature, both in its support and service.[6]

No Proof-Texts or Cliches. A woman once said this about the famous holiness evangelist E. Stanley Jones: "Apart from the Holy Spirit, Brother Stanley would be a *mess*." Jones humbly reports in his autobiography: "But with the Holy Spirit I am not a mess, but a *message*."[7] What a difference! Jones was a living *Yes* to the world because God had first said a redeeming *Yes* to him. Holiness is a way

---

[5] D. Michael Henderson, *John Wesley's Class Meeting*.
[6] Jonathan S. Raymond, *Social Holiness: The Company We Keep*.
[7] E. Stanley Jones, *Song of Ascents*.

of life, a manner of speaking, rather than so many biblical proof-texts and clever spiritual cliches. It's love's spoken-out and acted-out substance, God's intention and provision for all his children.

There are those times when speaking to or about the holy God exhausts our human ability. Paul says, "So here I am, preaching and writing about things that are way over my head, the inexhaustible riches and generosity of Christ" (Eph. 3:8). God will come in God's own time and way, once as small as a child and eventually bigger than life as the reigning Lord of all creation. While the joy of that final day will be thrilling, the full reality will be inexpressible! Sometimes our best speaking is to fall reverently silent. The sounds of timely silence can be thrilling indeed.

The great responding "Yes!" so needed in the church today is our hearty acceptance of the call of God for the holiness of his people. This is speech that expresses faith in the holy God who has offered a cleansing gift and a godly way of life, one of holy love. Here are great hymn lines from Charles Wesley, speech almost beyond human words, speech worthy of constant Christian use:

> Love divine, all loves excelling,
> Joy of heaven to earth come down;
> Fix in us Thy humble dwelling,
> All Thy faithful mercies crown.
> Jesus, Thou art all compassion,
> Pure, unbounded love Thou art;
> Visit us with Thy salvation,
> Enter every trembling heart.

Biblical holiness does not assure perfection of our life performance, but at least it's a genuine crossing of the threshold. We are promised that "when we shall see him we *shall be like him* (1 Jn. 3:2). The biblical holiness message is not based on a few isolated proof texts of Scripture. The atoning work of Christ is fundamental and adequate for our deepest spiritual needs, both for time and eternity. The truth of that work is so profound that always we will be reaching out to comprehend and appropriate it more and more fully. It's so central to biblical revelation that it appears in some form on most pages of the sacred text. When the holy God speaks, the very words are holy.

Exploring The Biblical Text

James 1:19-26. We believers must be quick to listen, being both hearers and doers of God's Word, while always guarding our tongues. "What goes into someone's mouth does not defile, but what comes out" (Matt. 15:11). We must never seek to demean or control each other by clever speaking. "Little children, let us love, not in word or speech, but in deed and truth" (1 Jn. 3:18). Here's something else we must never do. "Those who say, 'I love God' and hate a brother or sister are liars, for those who do not love those they have seen cannot love God whom they have not seen" (1 Jn. 4:20).

2 Timothy 4:16-18. Holy speech is truth sharing and love expressing, an overflow "in the Spirit" of what God has placed deep in the heart. Paul reports to Timothy from prison that he had been rescued from the lion's mouth, the world of unholy speech, and been enabled to proclaim the gospel of Christ so that all the Gentiles could hear it. Therefore, "to God be the glory forever and ever. Amen!"

Enriching Our Understanding

The Language of Love. "God being our helper, speak nothing harsh or unkind to each other. The sure way to avoid this is to say all the good we can, both of and to one another. In all our conversation, either with or concerning each other, we should use only the language of love, speaking with all softness and tenderness, with the most endearing expression which is consistent with truth and sincerity."[8]

Beyond our speaking tone always should be an announcement of the right spiritual season of the year, springtime. "There is divine light arriving, a warm sun shining, a grace-full rain falling. New life is possible, even inevitable if requirements are met. We are to open ourselves to the warm sun and gentle rain. Regardless of negative circumstances, joy is now very realistic. The wintertime grip of sin and death should begin to melt away. God is here and has loved us

---

[8] John Wesley, *Letter to a Roman Catholic.*

with an everlasting love."[9] That's the kind of holy speech so many need to hear.

Controlling the Speaking Agenda. We must be careful not to allow the world around us to control all conversations. If it's allowed to set the speech agenda, we'll always find ourselves stumbling awkwardly to answer its skeptical questions. Jesus often faced trick questions that tried to force him into an accuser's speech corner. The right questions tend to have amazing answers that confound selfish human minds. Curiosity will drive questions about the biology of the birth of Jesus and the mechanics of his miracles. Don't strive to come up with clear and final answers that try to express the inexpressible.[10] Stay humble and speak love.

A Call To Action

In the initial chapters of his letter to the Romans, Paul attempts to explain his complex theological thoughts—many words not always easily followed. What then would be the best way for him to end this complex work of theology? It's with heartfelt emotion that communicates well to all. The most appropriate thinking about godly things must come down to the pure adoration of God. It must allow the intellectual exercise of deep thinking to yield to a rich relationship of divine grace received and fellowship experienced.

Paul concludes with: "To the only wise God, through Jesus Christ, be the glory forever. Amen!" (Rom. 16:27). Is that your personal witness, your message to the world? If so, your tongue is sanctified! All good theology and quality Christian testimony are best expressed in acts of worship.[11] The divine news coming in Jesus Christ is more than analytical argumentation with technical words. It's to be our amazement that melts into "doxology," our lives centered around praising God. Do you sense that and will you yield to it, kneel before it, and speak often and with courage about it?

---

[9] *A Year with Rabbi Jesus*, vol. 2, week 7.
[10] *A Year with Rabbi Jesus*, vol. 2, week 4.
[11] Geoffrey Wainwright, *Doxology*.

The Ultimate Diet

What's a good way to protect the holy temple of God? By eating a holy diet. The appetizer is intentional silence—"Be still and know that I am God" (Ps. 46). Be silent long enough that God may be heard speaking. "He who has an ear, let him hear what the Spirit says to the churches" (Rev. 3:20–22). Instructs Jesus, the main course of a holy meal is "Do this in remembrance of me." The best item on the holiness menu is, "Be cleansed by the blood of the cross and nourished by the Bread of life." Come to the table. It's supper time!

Enjoy the Holiness Meal Served by the Lord. Christian Holiness is . . . Dieting on the Food of Jesus. Luke 22:19-20; John 4:34-35

The Bible often speaks of bread and wine, milk and honey, fish and olives. Almond trees were abundant. The Hebrew word for almond also means "watchful," so the almond represents God's watchfulness over his people. During the first centuries after Christ, Christians used a fish symbol to denote secret meeting places to safely identify friends and worship God. Jesus occasionally spoke of food. He assumed that the purity of the individual is connected with the purity of things regularly consumed. He attached holiness to a meal—"Do this in remembrance of me."

Christians were freed from many of the traditional Jewish restrictions on the eating of particular foods, although there was an early struggle of some believers over whether to "abstain from food sacrificed to idols" (Acts 15:29). If meat had been given to some idol and then sold in the marketplace, was it religiously tainted? Some Jesus people would buy and eat, meat is just meat after all, and some would not. Paul saw no problem with such eating but cautioned about using freedom in a way that injured "weaker" believers. Flaunting freedom can be failing to love.

It's important to think of "diet" as more than trying to lose weight. A spiritual diet is eating properly in order to live well. Pursuing Christian holiness is reaching for life's best by liberally sampling God's best. Not only does partaking of the divine life yield health for our own souls. As we take in our share of the life of God's Spirit, we can begin to bear divine fruit in the traffic of public life. We become a source of spiritual nourishment for the world.

Christians should eat well, come themselves to taste good, and finally feed others who hunger for such dietary richness. Too many Christians project negativity toward those outside the church (Gal. 5:15). They give the impression that religion is restrictive, sour tasting, maybe necessary but hardly desirable. There is nothing more damaging to the Christian cause than a poor diet and its upsetting social results. Christian holiness is being well nourished by the Spirit and thus able to be nourishment to others with serious dietary problems.

The Best on Heaven's Menu. Kindness is the meat in the holy sandwich of Christian living, while love and self-control slices that hold the sandwich together. Inside are other luscious ingredients, like the best of joy, peace, patience, generosity, faithfulness, and gentleness. The result of eating such a meal is nourishment to the soul that surpasses anything available in any human restaurant. It's the menu of heaven, and every child of God ought to be enjoying such a rich and colorful feast. To order anytime, just ask for the Bread of Life, and you'll get it all! It's found on the menu under "JESUS."

Hubert Harriman ministers to Christian missionaries serving in several countries. His great concern "is that we send only those who know the holiness of God in the fullness of the Holy Spirit, the fire of the Holy Spirit, the focus of the Holy Spirit, and the fruit of the Holy Spirit."[1] Maybe international representatives of the faith need to be ultimate dieters, especially full of divine and delicious fruit. However, all Christians are to be on mission whatever the geography, and thus they should be praying:

> My Father in heaven, please nourish me with living water and the real bread of life. May the true bread, your Son Jesus, cause me to grow and be strengthened so that I can bear good fruit to nourish a world hungering for hope. Be my personal menu, Lord. If we are what we eat, let me become more like you, meal by meal. Keep me from feeding on the perennial bad food of the church's ceremonialism, creedalism, and legalism. Cold externals are hardly the spices of life or the ingredients of effective evangelism.

Stop Eating Spoiled Food! There's something both tempting and toxic about feeding greedily on the world's goods. When we're thirsty, we should drink clean water. When hungry, we should stop eating spoiled food since wholesome spiritual food is readily available. Serious followers of Jesus intentionally position themselves to receive the bounty of God, the sustenance of sanctification. Christian holiness is putting oneself at the table of the Lord and humbly asking to be fed.

Daniel refused to eat the rich food of the imprisoning empire (Dan. 1). John was imprisoned on a desolate island (and writing the Book of Revelation) because the food of the Roman Empire sickened the soul. We must "seek the Lord" wherever we are or we will get cooked in the fires of others. Jesus is the true Bread of Life.

---

[1] Hubert P. Harriman and Barry L. Callen, *Color Me Holy*.

When he is available, and he is right now and always, why go for the moldy crusts on the world's tables? Bigger barns only set the stage for bigger collapses. Greedily eyeing the neighbor's goods is step one to going blind. Gorging on the fat of the land eventually will disrupt bodily functions and compromise the health of the soul.

To be mature disciples of Jesus, eating habits and a genuine life change are necessary. The results are fruit-bearing and life-nourishment sharing. The required change involves a cleansing newness of life at its center. Christian holiness is both a wonderful *now reality* and a *lifetime quest*, a journey from fallen lostness to restored wholeness, from spiritual malnutrition to deep soul health. We're being invited to come and be fed from the menu of life prepared from the riches of heaven, with the divine Host graciously joining us at the table (Rev. 3:14-22).

The Supreme Meal. Jesus told his disciples to eat regularly from the feast he was providing. This partaking of the "Lord's Supper" encourages spiritual progress and development of the "fruit" of the Spirit. This fruit is comprised of the holy character traits of a mature, well-fed Christian. This common meal has become sacred for Christians worldwide because it dramatically recalls Christ's work and anticipates the heavenly banquet he is preparing for the well-fed faithful. Found in 1 Cor. 11: 20–34 are the three nourishing dimensions of this supreme supper of the Lord. This meal of all meals is . . .

1. **Sanctifying**. The Lord's meal includes a series of remembrance symbols. To remember in the biblical sense is to become vitally *involved* in the reality being remembered, in this case the death and resurrection story of Jesus Christ. To be holy is to be actively extending the benefits of Christ's sacrificial death by now becoming like Christ and his servant life through personal experiencing of the power of his resurrection.

2. **Social**. To be holy also involves social implications that emerge from being Christlike (Gal. 3:28). An essential part of the fruit of the Spirit is "discerning the body" when we eat and drink at the Lord's table. We gladly affirm all who

choose to eat and drink with us, past and present, in our land and far away, of our color and culture or of any other. To be holy is to be engaging in the righting of relationships and the forming of a new and inclusive community like the world does not know. It's the church, the body of Jesus.

3. **Seditious**. To be in Christ and part of the Christ community at the table of the Lord is to participate in a *new creation*. It's to declare ultimate allegiance to Jesus Christ, joining his spiritual force that's working within the world to undermine its false values and renew it in the image of Christ's love and justice. To be holy is to deliberately and joyfully hold membership in a higher order, to pledge allegiance to the heavenly King who is above all earthly kings.[2]

Feasting and Fasting. Feasting at the Lord's table should be balanced by what seems like the opposite, a fasting that temporarily refrains from eating. The point of Christian fasting is to gather spiritual strength and resources. It's a planned abstaining that's an act of spiritual *affirmation*. It's a positive way of waiting on God that can bring increased awareness of the spiritual dimensions of life and their nourishing gifts.

Fasting, rather than a renunciation of life, is a means of releasing new life within. It's a form of self-death resulting in spiritual resurrection. As the Spirit of God gains possession of our attention and hearts, testimony is freshly received that we really are children of God (Rom. 8:16), children intended ourselves to be food for the world.

At least as much is said in the Bible about *fasting* as about *giving*. One enables the other. The missionary activity of the church began in Antioch when Barnabas and Saul were commissioned: "Then after fasting and praying, they laid their hands on them and sent them off" (Acts 13:3). While "diet" is generally assumed to mean unwelcome self-denial, Christian fasting is a willing exhaling of the temporarily distracting so that we can begin inhaling fresh winds of the Spirit. It's a means of becoming spiritually full, of reaching for more of the nourishing holiness offered by God.

---

[2] See Elaine Heath, *Five Means of Grace*, and the chapter "Exercising the 'Means' of Grace," in Barry Callen, *Catch Your Breath!*

Exploring The Biblical Text

Luke 22:19-20. Jesus took a cup and, after giving thanks, said, "Take this and divide it among yourselves." Then he took a loaf of bread, gave thanks, broke it, and gave it to them, saying, "This is my body, which is given for you, do this in remembrance of me." What a divine meal, and yet what misunderstanding there was. Immediately after the disciples did as instructed, they began to argue among themselves about who was the greatest. Here's what they should have understood and affirmed with each other.

The consumers of this meal of the Lord are to be the humblest and yet the boldest of humans. They are to be the holy ones who follow the eating and drinking with thanksgiving and life-sharing. To be holy is to abandon the pecking orders of this world by receiving the new life of Jesus through abandonment of pride and self-promotion. It's to follow the advice of David to his son Solomon. "Be strong and courageous. Don't be afraid or discouraged, for the Lord God is with you. He will not fail or forsake you" (1 Chron. 28:10-30).

> Trust no Future, howe'er pleasant.
> Let the dead Past bury its dead.
> Act--act in the living Present!
> Heart within, and God o'erhead![3]

John 4:34-35. Christian holiness often is confined to having some kind of elevated spiritual experience. It is that, to be sure, but such an experience, wonderful as it may be, soon can sour and become virtually meaningless, even self-serving. It must be accompanied by a distinctive pattern of life actions that focus around actually doing the Lord's will. Holiness is being new and doing newly, knowing and actively representing the truth with humility and courage.

Jesus said that his food was to do the will of his Father who sent him. He followed that by pointing out that the world is ripe for harvesting. The holy ones are those who really belong to Jesus and his ingathering mission. They gladly share the Master's food and use its strength to become harvesters, finding the lost, feeding the hungry, pointing the spiritually deprived to the available feast of heaven.

---

[3] Henry Wadsworth Longfellow, "A Psalm of Life."

Enriching Our Understanding

The Bread of Life. Being filled at the Lord's table is recalling and being enriched by the redeeming Word of God in Christ, made dramatically visible at the cross. Wrote Charles Wesley, "And lo! My Lord is here become the *Bread of life* to me."[4] Therefore,

> Make our earthly souls a field
> Which God delights to bless;
> Let us in due season yield
> The fruits of righteousness.
> Make us trees of paradise,
> Which more and more Thy praise may show,
> Deeper sink, and higher rise,
> And to perfection grow.[5]

Digesting with Joy. "The Christian life is to be less one of a divine law being forced down our throats by an authoritarian God and much more an opening to life offered by a grace-filled and most generous God. The people of the New Covenant obey because they are in a relationship with God that they have consciously and freely accepted. They are coming to really 'know' God, and thus are finding obedience natural and life-giving. Commandments there will be, but the yoke of obedience will be easy and its burden light (Matt. 11:30). Death to self opens the door to a spontaneous life eternal."[6]

A Call To Action

The invitation has come. The heavenly banquet is spread and your seat is reserved. Will you arrive? While there is no advance cover charge, this meal will cost you everything, and bring you even more! On the table is the fruit of life itself that will nourish you and then, through you, nourish others. You are to come and receive, then go to serve. You are to regularly return to the Lord's table. It's here that all the faithful remember what the Lord has done and come to share in his crucifixion death and resurrection life.

---

[4] Elaborated by T. Crichton Mitchell in *Charles Wesley*.
[5] Charles Wesley, "Us Who Climb Thy Holy Hill."
[6] Barry Callen, Steve Hoskins, Jonathan Powers, *A Year with Rabbi Jesus*, vol. 2, week 22.

The Lord's supper is a feast without equal. Don't be late! Once fed richly by the Spirit, and in fellowship with the whole body of Christ, let your heart sing these words with the whole church:

> One holy name she blesses,
> Partakes one holy food;
> And to one hope she presses,
> With every grace endued.[7]

Come, eat and drink at the one table where there is a *fact* and a *promise* that can change your world. *The Fact*: the bread of God is the bread that comes down from heaven and gives life to the world (Jn. 6:33). *The Promise*: Jesus declared, "I am the bread of life. Whoever comes to me will never go hungry, and whoever believes in me will never be thirsty (Jn. 6:35). To be holy is to be well-fed by the food and drink of heaven.

---

[7] Charles W. Naylor, "The Church Has One Foundation."

Please Don't Call Me "Christian"!

It's sad but true. The church of Jesus carries a lot of unholy baggage from its past. Holiness rests only in the blessed being and name of God, not in given church institutions and cherished religious programs formed to try representing the Master. While in myself I am nothing special, I would like to be identified with the One for whom I need give no excuse. We believers are judged by our labels and affiliations. I want the Lord's name over my door. I love the church, even with all her spots and wrinkles, but I prefer to be identified primarily with the Lord of the church who is pure and perfect.

The Followers of Jesus were Called "Christians." Christian Holiness is . . . Aspiring to the Best of Identities. Acts 11:26; Ephesians 2:19-20

The following may seem surprising, even a little shocking, but it shouldn't be. I have not abandoned my faith and converted to something entirely new. To the contrary, the living of life, coupled with long study of the fields of Christian theology and church history, have deepened my faith, while also bringing me some cautionary lessons. One lesson leads me to this. I request that people avoid calling me "Christian." In our compact world today, with its many faith traditions squeezed together, Christianity as an institutionalized faith carries so much baggage that confuses and even corrupts the public view. My wife and I recently were on a tour bus in the Caribbean. Someone asked what churches were on the island. The guide started with "Catholic, Anglican, Moravian, Adventist, Pentecostal, Salvation Army, and more." He added a bit sarcastically, "Each has its tarnished reputations and struggles."

Was Jesus a Jew? Of course. A Pharisee, Sadducee, Zealot, Essene, or other segment of Judaism? As far as we know, he loved them all, at times was severely critical of each, and formally belonged to none. He hadn't come to destroy his beloved tradition but to reform it in fundamental ways. He wished it to rise above its checkered history to its intended fulfillment. Being mired in the "traditions of the elders" was no longer adequate.

Can we relate to the bewildering crush of Christian identities somewhat like that? As I read church history, I am pleased at the visions and distressed at some of the implementations. I'm the same as an individual believer. I aim high and hit whatever I hit. Holiness is my goal; humanity is my limiting context.

The Baggage I Don't Want. "Christianity" as a formal religion is not something found in the New Testament, although the word did appear in Antioch. It was a designation not commonly used until at least the second century. A Roman emperor decided around 315 A.D. that it was to his political advantage to adopt the Jesus movement of Judaism as his very own. Many religious historians now see the faith having "fallen" into serious compromise with such a political affiliation. Jesus people had become unholy wards of the Empire.

It's a sad fact. Much that is part of the "Christian" world today is not worth supporting or being associated with by a serious believer in Jesus. Indeed, it may be better to be known simply as a dedicated disciple of Jesus than be painted with a broader "religious" brush with its particular creeds, institutions, rules, and checkered histories. "It cannot be denied that too often the weight of the Christian movement has been on the side of the strong and the powerful and against the weak and oppressed—this, despite the gospel."[1]

To take the general name "Christian" usually requires explaining what is *not* meant, and often leads to adding strategic adjectives—"I'm a liberal, fundamentalist, ecumenical, pentecostal, Eastern, Western, or whatever Christian." There's no end to names, nuances, and confusions. It's a complex and burdensome business, one rarely helpful to the Jesus cause. There may be merit in going back to the New Testament accounts of Jesus and focusing one's present identity more directly on his actual person and recorded teachings than with all that people carrying various Jesus-related designations have been and done and insisted upon since.

What Do I Want? I prefer to lessen the divisive process of explaining the "kind" of Christian I am and distance myself as much as possible from the terrible misdeeds of some past representatives of the Jesus faith (the crusades, support for slavery, persecution of Jews, cooperation with dictators, etc.). I prefer not to be trapped by a given creedal tradition of the faith that has both its strengths and inevitable frailties.[2] Accomplishing this is hard, I know, but it's a holy quest I choose to attempt.

"Denominations" tend to be tribal and artificially narrow the Christian fellowship, unfortunately lessening its cooperation in mission. Formal and mandatory creeds tend to stifle searching after the fuller truth and the best contemporary ways of expressing it. Religious labels tend to stereotype unfairly and isolate believers unnecessarily from others in the faith. I hope to step outside this narrowing

---

[1] Howard Thurman, *Jesus and the Disinherited*.

[2] The concern here is hardly new. This reforming impulse among Christians is traced in Barry Callen's *Radical Christianity* and also in Howard Snyder's *The Radical Wesley*.

"sectism." I'm even inclined to step a little outside the "Holiness" tradition that I love, thinking it more "holy" to put some distance between myself and all the divisive legalisms and organizational splintering that have troubled this wonderful Christian tradition.

The name "Jesus" is the Greek for the Aramaic "Yeshua." A young man from Nazareth was called by this name because he was *God with us*, come to save (Lk. 2:21). Mary's song of praise reports that Jesus came to "scatter the proud, bring down the powerful, fill the hungry with good things, and send the rich away empty" (Lk. 1:51-53). Accordingly, I now am seeking to be known only, or at least primarily, as a sincere "Follower of Jesus." I hope to be motivated by the wisdom and power of Christ's Spirit, seeking to continue in my small way to join in what Jesus came to do. It's a holy quest in a holy cause led by the Holy Spirit.

God's Church Intention. The church is to be the common fellowship and united mission of all people deeply committed to Jesus Christ. Such people have been changed by the power of Christ's Spirit, hunger daily for a further maturing of their spiritual experience, and seek ways of being active instruments of the ongoing ministry of Jesus. Disciples of Jesus are the "saints" of God who together form God's church, regardless of the names of their specific religious affiliations.

The worthy goal, the holy quest, is for all believers to become known primarily for being seized by a vision of God's people as one united and living family, humble and tolerant enough to keep growing and learning, and daring enough to face the rich and powerful of the world and feed the poor and abused in Jesus' name.

I don't want to be known as an adherent of some section of Christians who sit smugly in a corner and look critically at all others who understand differently a point or two of Christian doctrine or practice. I want to be identified more directly with the name of Jesus, with all his people, and with a reaching for the fullness of the truth that's in him. I don't want to be labeled with all that's been called "Christian" over the centuries. I want to keep moving beyond the common compromises of highly institutionalized churches and a tragically divided Christian world. Will you join in this holy quest?

Maybe we can't know a book by its title, but a proper title at least is a good place to begin. Effective evangelism requires moving from fine talk about the church to a real *being* of the church in its intended holiness and unity. No group of believers has a corner on all truth. Authority lies in the biblical revelation of God in Jesus Christ, not in the interpretations and traditions of any one body of believers. So, please just call me a humble follower of Jesus. Lead me, Lord!

"Let Me See Jesus Only!" is a great song title.[3] Can we become known as believers trying to do just that? The center of Christian faith is Jesus Christ, not an identifying with all the history, structures, and creeds that have carried the name "Christian." The faith derives its life and meaning from Jesus who was none other than God with us, true holiness seen in flesh, our Master and model. We are to be citizens of the "kingdom" (reign) of God rather than of any human "empire," religious or not.

This desire is to "bless the Lord, and all that is within me bless his holy name" (Ps. 103:1). Why? "For the Mighty One has done great things for me, and holy is his name" (Lk. 1:49). We should pray as the Lord directed. "Our Father in heaven, hallowed be *your name*." "Hallow" is in the active voice, meaning that by our very lives we are to seek to make God's name known as holy. Hearts that have been brushed with the gentle colors of God's holiness are now to honor a holy God in such a high and holy way.

Exploring The Biblical Text

Acts 11:26. The hand of God was with the early apostles as they proclaimed the good news of Jesus, and many became believers (11:21). Barnabas, "full of the Holy Spirit and faith," was sent to Antioch. Saul also was brought there and for a year they met with the church and taught many people. It was there that early believers were first called "Christians." The meaning of the word involves "reflecting the family characteristics of the Christ." To be an obvious member of the family of Jesus, part of the body that is his church, is to function as Jesus would in ways that are noticed and deeply appreciated by others. That's how we believers ought to be known.

---

[3] Composed by W. Dale Oldham.

Ephesians 1:3-18. The stories of our church labels and organizations have their place and meanings, of course, but they go wrong when given too much emphasis. Paul declares that God's activity in Christ is the big story that transcends all time and space and other stories. Our eyes are drawn to this grand picture from which true blessings flow. The early chapters of Paul's letter to Ephesus drip with thanksgiving and joy at the great blessing God is to his people. In fact, how lavish indeed are God's gifts to humankind.

This New Testament text echoes loudly the classic words of the Westminster Larger Catechism. The chief end of human life is "to glorify God and to enjoy him forever." God is eternal and now is with us in the birth of Jesus to show us who he is eternally. God always has been choosing us and ready to provide us with full life in him (forgiveness and holiness). We were in God's loving heart before the creation even was. The church is not the social structures we humans build around our faith but "the household of God that is built on the foundation of the apostles and prophets, with Christ Jesus himself as the chief cornerstone" (Eph. 2:19-20).

Enriching Our Understanding

The True Religion. True religion cannot be evaluated merely by right *thinking* or right *doing*, for the outward activities of both mind and life can belie the heart's true inward condition. In John Wesley's view, true religion can neither be reduced to *orthodoxy* (having the right system of beliefs or opinions), nor to *morality* (the outward practice of justice, mercy, and truth), nor to *formality* (attending to all the outward observances of religious practice without the inner reality). These three characteristics all belong to true religion and can be conducive to it, but by themselves fall short. True religion, when it's "real" religion, refers to having the inward reality of a *transformed heart* that can give rise to the proper outward expressions of religious life.[4] Can the church focus its identity and mission on true religion?

---

[4] Philip R. Meadows, in Callen and Thorsen, *Heart & Life*.

God's Presence Our Light. An ancient Irish poem was rediscovered in the early twentieth century. It puts proper stress on the importance of the lordship of Jesus Christ and our singular devotion to him. The verses combine the images of heart worship, the indwelling presence of Christ, and God as the high king of heaven, all calling the believer to the deepest of personal relationships with the Savior. Beyond labels and human affiliations, this higher, holy calling is the heart of everything.

> Be Thou my vision, O Lord of my heart;
> naught be all else to me, save that Thou art.
> Thou my best thought, by day or by night;
> waking or sleeping, Thy presence my light.

A Call To Action

To be a conscious member of the body of Christ, not merely a fragmented part but the whole body, requires a broad vision and an intentional end to the arrogance of particular church organizations. We are tribal people by instinct, but Jesus calls us to be intentional members of the whole family of Jesus. The divine gifts of all church members are to function for the good of each member, and whatever gifts each may have are for the enrichment of the whole body.

Are you ready to look and step outside the little corner of the faith community where you happen to be? Don't necessarily leave, just raise your sights. Dare to be a world Christian, a whole-church member. Whatever our differing gifts and experiences and affiliations, I need you and possibly you need me. Let's be one people in Christ, united in mission for Christ, holy ones together because of Christ.

> Every Christian has a legacy in every other Christian. We receive that legacy only as we receive each other and relate, moving eagerly beyond group boundaries. We must re-examine the boundaries imposed by denominational differences and distinctions in the attempt to understand and live out the imperatives of Christian unity.[5]

---

[5] James Earl Massey, *Views from the Mountain*, B. Callen and C. DeYoung, eds.

God calls us to a crucial, difficult, and holy quest. It's all based on this:

> The church's one foundation is Jesus Christ, her Lord;
> she is his new creation, by water and the Word.
> From heav'n he came and sought her, to be his holy bride;
> with his own blood he bought her, and for her life he died.
>
> Elect from ev'ry nation, yet one o'er all the earth;
> her charter of salvation, one Lord, one faith, one birth.
> One holy name she blesses, partakes one holy food,
> and to one hope she presses, with ev'ry grace endued.[6]

How Should the Church be Holy?

How are difficult decisions to be made by Christians? Judgments should come through the three root metaphors common to the whole message of the New Testament. The church is to (1) embody a manner of life that shows the redemptive purposes of God. It is to do this (2) in the manner of the cross of Jesus, joining the fellowship of his sufferings (Phil. 3:10), with church members bearing each other's burdens (Gal. 6:2). When living like that, the church will (3) reflect as it should the power of the resurrection of Jesus in the middle of an unredeemed world.

—See Richard B. Hays, in the
Moral Vision of the New Testament

---

[6] These hymn lyrics are by S. J. Stone.

Surviving Upside Down

Holiness is a winning by losing. It's becoming a willing member of the Upside-Down reign of God. To be holy is to be whole and fully alive by taking the extended hand of Jesus and walking humbly by his side through this life and later into another that's better yet. While this is wisdom at its best, in the eyes of the world it's sheer foolishness. It's carrying a cross rather than seeking applause. It's the costly risk of accepting death as maybe the way to real life. Regardless of the misunderstanding, reverent submission is the path to dignity and true freedom.

We're Invited to a Cross Death that's Life-Generating. Christian Holiness is . . . Embracing the "Unconventional" God. John 12:20-33; Hebrews 5:5-10

It clearly is the truth, and often its results, awkward and unusual, will have to be accepted. The ways of God are hardly "conventional," rarely predictable, sometimes the opposite of what we humans typically expect or want. God seems to specialize in the counter-cultural. His kingdom is upside down.[1] The creation has gone wrong. Its typical ways now are hardly what God intends. Recall these famous words of poet Robert Frost:

> I shall be telling this with a sigh
> Somewhere ages and ages hence:
> Two roads diverged in a wood, and I,
> I took the one less traveled by,
> And that has made all the difference.

Indeed. Choosing the path of life showing the least wear and filled with many unknowns is hardly the easy way to go. To join the kingdom of God is to be willing to overturn some things now accepted as "normal" by those who don't belong. There are questions and risks, natural hesitations and required faith.

Choosing God's reign may not be the most comfortable way to live, but it's the best way. "Jesus is leading us to the death of illusions, and illusions die hard. Jesus is leading us to the death of self-will, and self-will is a stubborn survivor. Jesus is leading us to the death of sin, and sin is a cat with nine lives. Jesus is leading us to the Lenten death that will catapult us into the Easter resurrection."[2] Will we choose to go that way? It seems so upside down. Holiness is hardly the path of ease.

How Odd of God. Sometimes it's said, "How odd of God to choose the Jews." They weren't more worthy or prone to success than anyone else. How strange and wonderful that God would now include you and me in the divine redemption plan, Jew or not. How unexpected it was that young David would be the one to overcome the giant Goliath. How strange indeed that the Ruler of the whole creation should appear as a helpless baby born in the worst of circumstances. To be holy is to yield to this divine strangeness and dare

---

[1] See the insightful book *The Upside-Down Kingdom* by Donald B. Kraybill.
[2] Eugene H. Peterson, *On Living Well*.

to reflect it in our own living. Like the Jews, we aren't worthy or special. We are loved and gifted by God, enabling the possibility of a "sanctified" life, one right-side up in an upside-down world.

John the Baptist shouts words of Isaiah to announce the advent of Jesus. He describes four surprises of this arriving kingdom, full valleys, flat mountains, straight curves, and level bumps (Lk. 3:4-6). The kingdom of God was coming near with the arrival of Jesus and would be different indeed. The dynamic reign of God wouldn't be a territory captured or particular place ruled, not a kingdom only *in* heaven but now present *from* heaven whenever women and men submit their lives to God's will. This kingdom of God is not merely a spirituality within given individuals but a collectivity, a network of persons who have yielded their hearts and relationships to the reign of God and the work of God's Spirit. It's the sanctified believer and church.

When learning about the Spirit of God in the Gospels, we encounter the "unconventional" God. Viewed through the lens of the life, death, and resurrection of Jesus, the Spirit tends to show up at odd times and in strange places, often with unusual teachings, including puzzling ones about birth from above and springs from below. The Gospels disclose what seems an alien world of the Spirit, a world that can mystify, challenge, and also invigorate.[3]

In the holiness leaders of the nineteenth century we encounter a "sanctified eccentricity," a living tradition on which to draw, one well-suited for us "post-moderns." We can "re-create the experiences of women and men who promoted the immediacy of God's presence for the sake of God's world. We must step outside the circles of ourselves in order to bring others into the larger circle of reconciliation. Eccencricity is the very nature of Christ."[4]

Rejoice in the "Unreasonable." The Spirit of God is the risen Jesus remaining with us as our comforter and guide. This divine presence is unlimited and unpredictable, like the wind that blows wherever it wills. It can exhibit tremendous power beyond our human ability to control. Such a humanly unmanaged divine reality

---

[3] Jack Levison, *An Unconventional God.*
[4] Douglas M. Strong, in Callen and Thorsen, eds., *Heart & Life.*

both thrills and sometimes frightens us. "For you," said Jesus, it "should be a joy, not a threat. That's because I've called you friends" (Jn. 15:15). The one thing we will never be is *in charge*. The unexpected, the counter-cultural, the other than our preference is always a possibility, a wisdom beyond our own.

Paul makes clear that our human partnership with God's working is a key indicator of whether divine grace has taken deep root in the church. The apostles had become "spectacles" to the world, "fools" for Christ (1 Cor. 4:9-10). Christian holiness apparently involves being willing to step forward and identify with God's acting, even though it's being viewed in public as unreasonable, abnormal, not smart or safe. Mature saints absorb gracefully being thought of as "fools." While apparently living upside down, they know that they have found the truly right-side-up life, the only one with a positive future.

The best way to stand confidently tall as a Christian is to kneel humbly low at the feet of Jesus. Giving up can be the door to total victory. Only when bowing down can one begin to see clearly and stand tall spiritually. The most likely way to become truly humble before God is to become truly alive in the Spirit. Christian holiness has been called the spiritual state of "deep time" when one becomes lost in God's love. In that lostness, so much is found.[5]

Leaning on Lent. The Christian season of Lent brings what sounds like unwelcome news. Living requires dying. Christians are called to follow the One who had to die if we were ever to really live. Rabbi Jesus made clear to his disciples that losing life is required if life is to be found. He showed the way by himself willingly suffering and becoming the source of new life for all who also would yield, accept the results of his saving work, and follow his life-death-life example. The possibility of eternal life exists only because of the self-sacrificing work of God in Jesus Christ and our self-sacrificing response to it.

The holiness message shines from 1 Samuel 17:1-49. David is the patron saint of underdogs. Who's fighting who? Is this the pathetic scene of a helpless shepherd lad with no conventional armor

---

[5] Richard Rohr, *Falling Upward.*

coming to battle against impossible odds? Yes, apparently, but that's hardly the point of this dramatic tale. The battle actually was God engaging the pantheon of no-gods, the humble champion of justice facing off against the overwhelming representatives of all injustice. Conventional wisdom said that disaster was just ahead. So much for such "wisdom."

The weapon of David's victory was an odd one indeed, little stones against a mountain of steel and muscle. The giant was a predator about to be devoured by the enslaved, the invincible conquered by the lowly. It was so unlikely an outcome, so unlike the real world. The odds are stacked against the helpless, those about to be exploited again. However, God loves the widows and orphans, the nobodies of the earth. The unconventional is way of love. The victory one day will be the Lord's, and that of his people, and that of the cause of justice and righteousness.[6]

Regardless of what may be preached on TV and sold in popular books, the holiness way of Christian faith is not the guarantee of upward social mobility, the glitter of success of the kind our world is so enamored. Rather, "it's the path of pain, the choice of downward mobility. It's the way that ends on a cross which, ironically, is the door to resurrection and eternal life."[7] If only today's church were filled with such upside-down wisdom!

God is setting upright our upside-down world. It's the logic of transformed life that appears silly to the selfish crowds of everyday. The constant need is for God's people to be filled with humble foolishness, life at its best, functioning with an eye focused on God's will. Holiness is a believer living a new life in Christ and speaking words of love and invitation that are more than religious double-talk that promises "happiness," even prosperity. The real message is way more upside-down than that!

Exploring The Biblical Text

John 12:20-33. Jesus speaks with a jarring proverb, probably not welcome but full of critical truth anyway. As with any seed,

---

[6] See Callen, Hoskins, Powers, *A Year with Rabbi Jesus*, vol. 2, week 37, "How Odd of God."

[7] Barry L. Callen, *Catch Your Breath!*

things must die in order to bear fruit (vs. 24). He calls his disciples to take up their crosses, die to their sinful selves, receive his gift of friendship and eternal life, and follow wherever led, strange and dangerous or not. Gaining the grand goal of his Father inevitably would involve for Jesus an arrest, torture, and finally execution. The Lord's attitude toward impending suffering and even death must come to be ours.

Only those prepared to give up everything will be in position to receive everything, eternal life for their time in this world and then forever. Discipleship with Jesus is hardly a safe or "normal" business, but always it will be bathed in love and is assured of a desirable future. When ridicule and persecution come, hold on until the resurrection morning arrives. The Father is pure love, evidenced dramatically by the self-emptying of Jesus on our behalf. He took the form of a servant even though he could have called a host of angels for protection (Phil. 2:4-7). If you want a picture of God, and one of your own calling in his service, read Isaiah 53.

Hebrews 5:5-10. This letter was written to encourage Christian believers to deepen their faith and thus become able to persevere in difficult times. Survival can happen only by realizing that living requires dying. By way of a cross, Jesus emerged as the very source of "eternal salvation for all who obey him" (vss. 5-9).

The Christian life is to be less one of law being forced down the throat by an authoritarian God and much more an opening of ourselves to new life offered by a grace-filled God.

The people of the new covenant obey because they are in a voluntary relationship with God whom they have consciously and joyfully accepted. They are coming to really know God, and thus are finding obedience natural and life-giving. They have moved from a mechanical religion to a vibrant, holy life. Commandments there will be, yes, but the yoke of obedience will be easy and the burden light (Matt.11:30). Death to self opens the door to the joys of life eternal.

Enriching Our Understanding

What's Actually Real? Happiness often is found in going the other way. Following Jesus is taking the road of life not usually traveled. We should come to church to be reminded of what's real. So many people live in artificial little worlds of their own making, or that someone dumped on them. Don't be taken in by fake news! It's truth standing awkwardly on its head, and it's everywhere and can sound quite correct. Because of Jesus, Christians have a quarrel with the world's definitions of reality. As disciples of Jesus, we are to align our lives with the new reality that Jesus calls into being. The world as it appears before our eyes may be more distracting shadow than actual truth. The truth is that the kingdom of God arrived with Jesus![8]

Finding the Full Truth. "When we Christian believers have finished our theologizing, we still shall not understand all mysteries. We are but human pilgrims following the pathways of knowledge, and to the end of the earthly way we shall still 'know in part.' And yet, our faith in Jesus Christ our Lord can give us the *assurance* of things hoped for, the *conviction* of things not seen. And is that not, after all, the object of the quest?"[9]

Robert Southey, author of the *Life of Nelson*, was a secular poet-laureate proposing to write a life of John Wesley. Could a man with literary but no spiritual gifts probe successfully the life of a spiritual giant like Wesley? He interviewed an old Methodist saint who thought the process impossibly upside down. "Sir, thou hath nothing to draw with, and the well is deep!"[10] Southey couldn't come up with the truth because he couldn't get down to find it!

A Holiness Prayer. We frail humans should pray like this. "I want to know and be committed to the truth, Lord, however it may relate to my expectation or personal preference. I want to be passionate in my faith, although short of being blindly fanatical. I'm

---

[8] Barry Callen and Steve Hoskins, *A Year with Rabbi Jesus*, vol. 1, week 14.
[9] Georgia Harkness, *Foundations of Christian Knowledge*.
[10] Quoted by James Stewart in *Walking with God*.

willing to be seen as "odd" if I'm sure it's Your way. I want to use my gifts for the good of the church and world, and not for my own advancement. If being with Jesus makes me "abnormal," help me not hesitate or be ashamed of the norm that You are, my God. Rid my soul of fear and fill it with awe and praise. If the boat I'm in is swamping, help me praise and not panic because I know that Jesus is onboard. When circumstances appear against me, help me remember who You are and whose I am."

A Call To Action

How can we find God? We don't have to! We only have to allow God to find us. That means to stop running away. Turn toward God in an attitude of expectancy. Act as though God *is*, and is with *you*, and with you *now*. Practice the presence of God.[11] Dare to choose the "odd" way of love and sacrificial living for others.

> Take my life and let it be, Consecrated, Lord, to Thee;
> Take my moments and my days, Let them flow in ceaseless praise.
> Take my will and make it Thine, It shall be no longer mine,
> Take my heart, it is Thine own, It shall be Thy royal throne.[12]

That's what it means to come alive in Christ, choosing to leave behind the old self, accepting a spiritual self-death, and claiming a spiritual life of set-apartness. It's to be committed to the Jesus way of life that doesn't shy even from the cross on the way to eternity. Are you ready for that?

Remember this wisdom from C. S. Lewis in the *Chronicles of Narnia*. After the decisive battle, Aslan, the great Lion, reports surprisingly that Prince Caspian now is able to assume his rightful kingship. But Caspian is uncertain about his readiness for such large responsibility. He's grateful but humble. Aslan then offers this telling judgment. "It's for that very reason that I know you are!" Humility is a clear mark of Christian maturity, a holy readiness for major responsibility, a low ready for high.

---

[11] E. Stanley Jones, *Abundant Living*.
[12] Hymn lyrics by Frances R. Havergal.

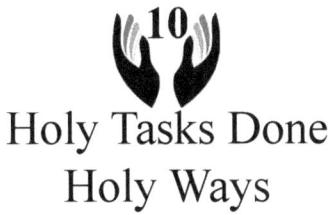

Holy Tasks Done Holy Ways

Swords and rockets or prayers and love? What methods of Christian ministry and evangelism are most appropriate? In church life we sometimes replace God with ourselves and our private agendas. We want to do God's things our own ways. We unconsciously mimic the secular singer Frank Sinatra who rather arrogantly crooned, "I've lived a life that's full, I've traveled each and every highway. And more, much more than this, *I did it my way*." That's Frank testimony, but God says, "It's certainly not the way for my people." God's things must be done *God's way*. Learning what that is and daring to do things that way is the path of Christian obedience. Holy tasks maintain their integrity only when done in holy ways. Perceiving which ways are holy requires living very close to the Spirit of all wisdom.

Holiness is the Way of Peace Rather than Those of Death. Christian Holiness Is . . . Life in Loving Service. Mark 8:31-38; Luke 1:79, 12:49-51

One Christian pastor sets the scene sharply. He says the Bible presents the Christian life not as a playground but a battleground. God has not saved us to live comfortably in suburbia. We are conscripted into God's army and have a commission from the Commander-in-Chief to take the saving message of Christ into enemy territory to win captives. Paul describes the Christian cause in such combative terms (Phil. 1:27–30). There will be struggle, opposition, a need to fight the good fight. With what weapons? Those of the Spirit (2 Cor. 6, Eph. 6, 1 Thess. 5).

Surely the work of the Lord must be done the Lord's way. Since Jesus came a "suffering servant," we must lower our worldly expectations about a warrior Messiah and the presumed promise of a victorious and prosperous church in our time. Jesus didn't call a host of angels to wipe out Rome, nor did he leave behind a fortune for his followers when his earthly end came. Jesus was a backwater Savior who sent out a landless group of disciples to give their lives away in selfless service.

How Should We Enter the City? Jesus had plans to steer a course toward Jerusalem. He knew that going there would invite a collision with the religious and Roman power establishments who were waiting. He pondered the plots against his life and knew that an ugly end was inevitable. No matter. He couldn't allow that to dominate his attention or dictate his actions. How would he enter the city? Riding on a lowly donkey, not leading an army of avenging angels!

Holiness is the high spiritual road traveled with the "low" methods of love that are prepared to suffer humbly as needed to serve the Master. Why did many of the first-century Jews reject Jesus as their Messiah? They weren't blind or stupid. They just couldn't accept the strange idea that their "Savior" would be hanged in humiliation by the hated Romans. Aren't pain and death signs of sickness and failure?

Frustrated with Jesus, Peter questioned how he was choosing to be the Messiah. "I'll use a sword if you won't!" (Mk. 8:32). The fact is that we'll never know what it means to be a Christian until we get straight how Rabbi Jesus insisted on being the Messiah, and it wasn't the way most of his people expected or wanted.

What of today? Has the icon of the swaggering cowboy John Wayne replaced the lowly Lamb of God?[1] Have contemporary "evangelicals" tended toward redefining the Messiah in the wrong image?

Paul announced a hard truth to the Philippian church. God "has graciously granted you the privilege not only of believing in Christ but of suffering for him as well" (Phil. 1:29). Suffering a privilege? Peter explains: "For to this you have been called because Christ also suffered for you, leaving you an example so that you should follow in his steps" (1 Pet. 2:20–21). Holiness is not avoiding or denying or being delivered from all of life's pain. The presence of the Lord in our lives sends us into the pain as carriers of healing and hope. The holy presence enables "an exhaling of selfish indulgence and then an inhaling of the fresh air of giving oneself away, an exchange that brings great spiritual gain."[2]

Suffering for Christ is not a sign of weakness. Martin Luther King, Jr., may have been abused and shot as he insisted on peaceful protest, but calling him "weak" is hardly appropriate. Thank God for the Holy Spirit and the reality of Pentecost. Thank God that Jesus did not leave us a powerless and anemic church! Love *is power*, just not the brutal kind.

The church is not to withdraw into some stagnant pool of detached self-righteousness. To the contrary, the church has a "political" mission that engages the world prophetically, just not with arrogance and coercion. It knows that its true nature and power lie in servanthood and not domination of others.

Being Counter-Cultural Peacefully. John Wesley was right. God's expressions of power toward us has focused on *empowerment* rather than control, manipulation, and overpowerment. We, then, are to walk in the world gently, peacefully, lovingly, and yet significantly. The Greek *eirene* (peace) appears in every New Testament book. It also should appear in the everyday actions of the disciples

---

[1] See Kristin Kobes Du Mez, *Jesus and John Wayne*.
[2] Barry L. Callen, *Catch Your Breath!*

of Rabbi Jesus. We have received and must share the peace of Christ. Doing so with violence violates Christ and his gospel mission.[3]

Being a follower of Jesus is clearly counter-cultural. Pride in nation, race, and family are honorable but cannot be elevated above our higher and holy citizenship in the kingdom of God. To champion the divine citizenship necessarily involves coming to the foot of Christ's cross and engaging in the painful sacrificing of all arrogance and selfishness. We people of Christ must be conscious of carrying a different passport, one issued by the kingdom of God.

Are Christians called to civil disobedience when loyalty to God is made impossible otherwise? Dare we sometimes do what those first apostles of Jesus did? Soon they were being flogged and commanded to shut up in public about Jesus (Acts 5:40). What happened? Considering it an honor to suffer for Jesus' sake, the disciples of the Risen Lord were barely beyond the door of the prison when they opened their mouths to start preaching again. "God," they confessed, "is our only authority."

Dietrich Bonhoeffer is a recent prophetic voice about the difficulty of knowing how to be Christian in extreme circumstances. He turned from a bright secular future to Christian ministry and then abandoned prominent ministry opportunities in the United States to return to the horrors of his beloved Germany in the 1930s. He knew suffering likely would follow if he opposed Hitler. He hated violence and yet finally joined a plot to kill Hitler. We learn much of his struggle from his *Letters and Papers from Prison*.[4]

Bonhoeffer once wrote that "the will of God is not a system of rules established from the outset." It must be found each new day as we walk faithfully in God's holy presence. We Christians know as we go, usually not in advance. Can we avoid reverting to violence even when victims of it? Will we insist on serving the holy cause in only holy ways? The church must not withdraw from public life and exist in a pool of detached self-righteousness. To the contrary, it has a "political" mission that engages the world, not with an agenda

---

[3] For the Christian approach to interpreting vengeance and holy war as found in the Old Testament, see Barry Callen, *Beneath the Surface*, 162-170.

[4] For the full story of Bonhoeffer's dramatic life and ministry, see Eric Metaxas, *Bonhoeffer: Pastor, Martyr, Prophet, Spy*.

of arrogance and coercion, but as a Jesus community that knows its true nature and realizes that its power lies in servanthood.

Timing is Important. We have received and must share the peace of Christ. Timing is important. It's not so much about *when* Jesus will come again as about when we will go announcing that he's *already here*. Go now! We always are to be ready for the Lord's coming again. Here's the best way to get ready for that grand day. Be busy about the Father's love-laced business *in the meantime*. Feed the hungry, shelter the homeless, and find the lost, spreading God's love abroad.

The best way to wait is to get up and go with Jesus, being like Jesus today! While we wait on our arriving King, the coming King also is expecting us to be building our lives around the qualities that characterize the current reign of God. There's a holy mission and it's to be pursued in holy ways. We are to be Jesus-like people reflecting the divine character and mission.

> A charge to keep I have; a God to glorify—
> A never-dying soul to save and fit it for the sky.
> To serve *the present age*, my calling to fulfill;
> O may it all my powers engage
> To do my Master's will.[5]

Read again Psalm 22:23-31. African-American spirituals like "Great Day" and "My Lord, What a Morning" reflect Christian people who know well great suffering and yet survive by declaring great faith in God right in the teeth of it all. In the face our shortcomings and many trials and temptations, holy Christians do more than lament the problems and confess their sins. They know it's time to praise God! After all, "the dominion belongs to the Lord and he rules over the nations" and all our personal circumstances (vs. 28). All who reverence the Lord should praise him! (vs. 1). Praise is a holy action that changes things and allows survival regardless.

---

[5] Hymn Title: "A Charge to Keep I Have" by Charles Wesley.

Exploring The Biblical Text

Mark 8:31-38. Peter just didn't get it. Jesus called him "Satan" and told him to get behind him. He had confronted Jesus about the very idea of his voluntarily culminating his messiahship by going to Jerusalem to face almost certain suffering and death. What Jesus was facing willingly made no sense to the impetuous Peter. The Master was distressingly plain in response. Any who would follow him would have a cross of some kind to face. Those refusing to embrace his way of being the Messiah one day would hear words of rejection from the Father's disappointed voice. The way of Jesus isn't the easiest of ways, it's just the only true way to be Christian.

Luke 1:79, 12:49-51. "Because of the tender mercy of our God, the dawn from on high will break upon us to guide our feet into the way of peace. I have come to cast fire upon the earth, and how I wish it were already ablaze! Do you think that I have come to bring peace to the earth? No, I tell you, but rather division!" These statements from Luke's Gospel appear in conflict with how Jesus handled Peter's call to violent action. Luke begins his life of Jesus by saying that the Lord would guide people into the ways of peace, but then adds in chapter twelve a darker part of the divine intention, one now reflected in the song *The Battle Hymn of the Republic*. It says God "hath loosed the lightening of his terrible swift sword."

While fire and division eventually may have to be the final means of divine judgment, it's not to characterize the ministries of the disciples of Jesus now. Followers of the Prince of Peace are to expose themselves to an experience of the fiery Pentecost of Christ's Spirit. That burning refines and restores souls into holy new creations, inspiring them to great deeds of love, righteousness, and self-sacrifice as instruments of the Spirit. The followers of Jesus are to be *holy* but not *harmless*, fully armed with the power of love (Eph. 6:13) and yet street-wise, prepared for anything (Matt. 10:16).

Enriching Our Understanding

Being Strong and Sweet. John Wesley construed God's power and sovereignty fundamentally in terms of *empowerment* rather than control or *overpowerment*. This does not weaken God's power but determines its character. As Wesley was fond of saying, God works "strongly and sweetly." That is, God's grace works powerfully but not irresistibly in matters of human life and salvation, empowering our *response-ability* without overriding our *responsibility*.[6]

The Spirit is Power. As Jesus was empowered, the church is empowered by the Spirit for its mission. That power must be at work in us (Eph. 3:20). The kingdom of God is not just a matter of talk but of power (1 Cor. 4:20). Outsiders ought to be able to sense the life-changing presence of Christ in one's witness (1 Cor. 14:25). God wants more than churches full of people. The great need is for people full of the Spirit.[7]

The New Testament concludes with a "political" message of Jesus. Revelation 5 portrays the slain and resurrected Lamb as the only one who can open the scroll. The Lamb therefore is worthy to receive praise and glory and power. It's the cross of Jesus that reveals the meaning of human history, not the sword of power politics. God's people are called to follow the Lamb wherever he goes. Like him, we are to "conquer" because of our politics of persevering love, not our recourse to coercion.[8]

I'll Lay Down My Life. A recent Christian prophet reported that he was speaking at a high-level meeting in South Africa when his emphasis on reconciliation was challenged as "too soft." He responded vigorously. "Reconciliation is not soft and namby-pamby. It is rugged and tough. The revolutionary says, 'The world is in trouble and I'm going to fix it. If you get in my way, I will kill you.' The reconciler says, 'The world is in bad shape and I'm going to work to change it. If you try to block me, I'm willing to lay down my life for the cause.' I then asked, 'Which of these two positions is soft and namby-pamby?' "[9]

There was a sharp difference of opinion among the first disciples of Jesus on how best to proceed. Simon the Zealot likely would

---

[6] Randy L. Maddox, *Responsible Grace*.
[7] Clark H. Pinnock, *Flame of Love*.
[8] See John Howard Yoder, *The Politics of Jesus*.
[9] Samuel G. Hines, *Beyond Rhetoric*.

have thought of Nathanael as too passive a pietist. One was a man of action, maybe even violent action as necessary, while the other focused on the devotional life and thought much about citizenship in the kingdom of God. Jesus called both of them to be his disciples, providing a composite model of social passion rooted in the spiritual life, not in a sword. He resolved the tension of contrasting methodologies "with a higher synthesis, the best of both, God's will done on earth as in heaven, with one hand up to God in worship and the other out to our brother man in service."[10]

A Call To Action

There are times when we who believe must stand for truth in the face of blatant untruth. God alone is to be praised and followed. We are to share God's love with everyone, regardless of their idolatries and unacceptable demands on us. Meanwhile, we must be careful not to become idolators ourselves. How easy it is to elevate personal thoughts and practices to the level of Christian truth. Too often we make fateful judgments about others based on our beliefs, and on occasion even are willing to resort to violence to force acceptance of our views.

"Happy are those who are able to promote peace and goodwill among men, and are therefore particularly engaged, as much as lies in them, to live peaceably with all."[11] Note these lyrics that mix power and patience, Christian humility and duty:

> Stand up, stand up for Jesus,
> Stand is His strength alone:
> The arm of flesh will fail you,
> Ye dare not trust your own.
>
> Put on the gospel armor,
> And watching unto prayer,
> Where duty calls, or danger,
> Be never wanting there.[12]

---

[10] James S. Stewart, *Walking with God*.
[11] John Wesley, *The Lord Our Righteousness*.
[12] Hymn lyrics by George Duffield.

Which Rules Am I To Live By?

Which actions of ours cause God to smile? It's seems hard to know. Equally sincere Christians have many different rules for right living. We know at least that we must avoid all that violates the known will of God. We must give up a selfish way of life, presenting ourselves as "living sacrifices" (Rom. 12:1-2). The psalmist gives us needed guidance. God's *love* is "to be ever before us" (Ps. 26). We are to discipline our lives around the law of love regardless of what religious rules seem good to us or are being pressed on us by others in church authority.

Holiness is Learning to Live by Love. Christian Holiness is . . . Being Open to the Spirit's Guidance. Psalm 16; Galatians 5:1, 13–25

Disciples of Jesus must avoid worldly distractions and preoccupations. Instead, we are to do something quite difficult. We are to live with the things of this world while not becoming addicted to them. It's the old "in it" but not "of it." That is, we are to be freed in Christ from slavery to things that are passing away while, in the meantime, not withdrawing from the world and failing to be responsible witnesses while yet in it.

The challenge is much like watching a professional sports game. It makes so much more sense when the rules of the game are well known. What constitutes a "foul" and what action puts points on the scoreboard? But what about trying to play the game when there are various editions of the rulebook in force at the same time? In the life of Christian faith, all the particulars aren't known in advance and some rules are general guidelines not always to be implemented the same way in different times and places. The Spirit of God is the needed interpreter of the demands of each moment.

Jesus was a Rule-Breaker. By the time of Jesus, the Jewish tradition had evolved numerous rules of precisely how the faithful should act in virtually every circumstance of life. To be pleasing to God, all rules were to be followed carefully. Jesus loved his heritage but proceeded to transform it in significant ways. One was to dispense with many of the religious rules when good sense or human compassion suggested acting otherwise. He made clear that an adequate fulfilling of the law was always practicing the *law of love*.

Rules can be cold, impersonal, and improperly limiting. They also can give security by making clear in advance what's to be done when particular circumstances come up. That way, no difficult decisions need to be made. Just follow the rule. By contrast, love is a marvelous law for life, highly personal but sometimes lacking in advance specificity about what should be done until a particular circumstance is faced. Each must be evaluated separately and fresh guidance from God received and followed.

Jesus was a master at love's applications. He violated various religious rules and paid a high price. It's difficult when there are no advance rules other than the law of love. That's why Christian holiness is so important. Life with the Spirit of Christ active within is the life capable of seeing circumstances through the Spirit's eyes and thus knowing how best to proceed.

The way of love must be Spirit directed. Too many Christian believers have diluted their understanding of holiness into something giving the public impression that lemons are the favorite fruit of the faithful. Belonging to the Father is not to wear a frown at every party. Paul emphasizes joy in his list of the spiritual fruit of God's Spirit. Joy is sandwiched in between love and peace (Gal. 5:23). Joy bursts forth throughout the pages of Scripture like geysers that cannot be suppressed. It fills the darkness with singing. Follow the rules of love and dance!

When some Pharisees told Jesus to quiet the praise of his disciples, he answered, "I tell you, if these were silent the stones would shout out!" (Lk. 19:40). They had learned to live joyously out of love. Jesus asked Levi, the hated tax collector, to walk with him. Being cozy with the world's riffraff can be as uncomfortable as it is appropriate, an obvious breaking of conventional religious rules. We are to look past the brokenness in people's lives and love them regardless of their unworthiness. Love and sing:

> Since Jesus gave all to redeem me, since only through mercy I live,
> It now is my joy and my purpose a whole-hearted service to give.
> I mean to live holy and blameless, a Christian indeed will I be.[1]

Christian holiness is being "possessed" by God. "Be in me increasingly so that your kingdom, your rule may guide my decisions, inspire my will, and determine my actions."[2]

Exploring The Biblical Text

Psalms 16. In moments of pain and confusion, so much depends on the believer having available a powerful memory of God's past actions. Such memory gives assurance and guidance to the present. What God wants of me now surely will be in line with what God has done and wanted in the past. In the stories of Elijah and Elisha, Jacob and Joseph, Moses and Aaron, the central message is that we

---

[1] Charles W. Naylor, select lyrics from his song "Wholehearted Service."
[2] Howard Thurman in his *Deep Is the Hunger*.

cannot manage alone. We need a community of faith to help us remember the promises of God. We need the church, the community of memory.

When we can think only of our pain and questions, companions in the faith can remind us of God's presence and promises. When we cannot sing, others can sing for us. When we cannot pray, others can carry the load. The theme of Psalm 16 reflects hymns such as "Great Is Thy Faithfulness," "Oh God, Our Help in Ages Past," and "God of the Ages, Whose Almighty Hand."

What about when there is no clear memory of what to do in a novel set of circumstances? What should happen when a decision must be made and there's no map, only wilderness with no GPS? The psalmist answers, "I bless the Lord who gives me counsel" (vs. 7). Beyond the church and Bible, when there are no guiding rules, we need the holy love and present ministry of God's Spirit.

Luke 9:59-62. Jesus gave would-be disciples some stern advice. My friends, dropping everything and following me isn't easy. Living by love has its challenges and risks. If you don't believe enough in me and my Spirit to take the risks, you had better stay home. You can't know it all in advance, you just can't. Love often has to be flexible and experimental in application. My Spirit won't give you a book of fixed rules, only a divine presence who always is prepared to show you the way, one step at a time, always in line with love.

Galatians 5:1, 13–25. The Galatian believers in Jesus lived in a world where the things we now take for granted, Christian customs, rituals, worship, a calendar for community celebration, even a written Scripture, were brand new or didn't yet exist. As a pioneering first-century community of faith, they lived with little or no tradition to ground their experience and direct their actions as Gentile Christians. It was like playing football with no sidelines to the field. It's difficult to know when you are out-of-bounds!

Authentic Christian discipleship requires both right beliefs and proper behaviors. If the Jewish law and the "traditions of the Elders" were no longer the safeguards against sin and the misuse of freedom, what was? Paul responds, "The Holy Spirit!" "Live by the

Spirit, I say, and do not gratify the desires of the flesh." There is one law, that of love. The whole law is summed up in a single commandment, "You shall love your neighbor as yourself" (5:14).

While God calls disciples to freedom, Paul announces a caution. "Do not use your freedom as an opportunity for self-indulgence" (5:13b). Believers must know that Christian holiness is not primarily two common things. It's not *asceticism* (denying ourselves to death) or *athleticism* (working ourselves to death). Instead, it's *acceptance*, allowing God's Spirit to love us into new, abundant, and finally everlasting lives that do the right because they love.

The Holy Spirit, once accepted, gifts and motivates believers to engage the world in ways that encourage hope of its returning to its intended wholeness of life. What rules are to be followed in this engagement process? No codebook is given, only a holy presence who points to holy ways of responding to possibilities as they emerge.

Enriching Our Understanding

The Rules of Being a Christian. Jesus Christ summarized all Christian commandments into just two: "Love the Lord your God and your neighbor as yourself" (Mk. 12:30-31). All other commandments are specific ways of trying to apply these as constructively as possible. Each Christian church fellowship may teach somewhat varying applications of these commandments, but all essentially agree that believers are to follow them as the Spirit of God directs. Jesus provides a series of specifics that give general guidance (Matt. 5-6).

Specifics of application, however, come only as one walks humbly with the Spirit along the paths of discipleship. "God calls us beyond merely 'doing right.' He calls us to be people who live in his way because we have his own heart (Jer. 32: 39). He calls us to be changed into his righteous people by the transforming power of his Holy Spirit. Right living results from the transformation of a person's mind and heart, rather than from any kind of self-imposed discipline."[3]

---

[3] Dennis Kinlaw, *The Mind of Christ*.

An Alternative to Empty Ritualism. While we all tend to denounce empty church ritualism, most of us need habitual practices that keep open our hearts and minds to God's transforming love. Without regular reminders we tend to drift away from God's missional call to love and serve our neighbors. John Wesley recognized five "means of grace," Christian spiritual practices that form a process of "going on to perfection." They are prayer, searching the Scriptures, the Lord's Supper, fasting, and Christian conferencing.[4] These disciplines are tools of the Spirit that serve well as divine guidance of behavior.

Beyond "Dermatology." Pharisees were the party of Judaism most keen on measuring spirituality by outward performance. The problem is that spiritual activity easily becomes a matter of habit and even ego more than expressions of the heart. Formal standards of religious activity become the litmus tests for holiness and righteousness. Others are then judged harshly when they don't conform to the set rules.

This mechanical and external preoccupation has been called specializing more in spiritual "dermatology" than "cardiology." The skin is kept clear while a heart attack is on its way. Jesus reacted against an obsession with outward cleansing valued over inward purity (Matt. 23:25-26).[5] Following him around, the disciples learned how inward purity reacts to new and demanding situations.

Here's wisdom worth pondering: "No mind can comprehend God's reality. If we approach God, we must advance not only by knowing but by *not knowing*. We must seek to communicate with God not only by words, but above all by silence in which there is only one word, and the one word is infinite love."[6] Why is a holy life in the Spirit of Jesus so important? Because there is so much we yet need to know and it's the Spirit who is sent as our life-long Teacher (Jn. 14:26).

---

[4] Elaine A. Heath, *Five Means of Grace*.
[5] Hubert P. Harriman and Barry L. Callen, *Color Me Holy*.
[6] Thomas Merton, *Love and Living*.

A New Freedom and Joy. Paul heralded a new freedom in Christ and was criticized sharply by some as a dangerous libertine. He understood the gospel of Christ to be marked by freedom, gratitude, and joy. It's the life of "I want to do this because of Christ" rather than "I will do this because I must." There's nothing more enslaving than trying to guarantee our acceptance with God by patterns of proper religious activity. Christians are to live as resurrection people who have an infectious testimony of fresh joy and really good news for all people.[7]

The good news is that we don't have to, in fact we can't earn our way to acceptance by God through our superior knowledge or constant right practices. The divine call is for us to be holy as God is holy, that is, to enter into a cleansing relationship with God through life in the Spirit. In that relationship we are reborn, reformed, gifted, guided, fulfilled, and sent. We finally will be judged not by our perfection of religious performance but by the presence of a personal relationship with Jesus Christ through the grace provided by his Spirit.

Paul made things quite plain to the Galatians in chapter five of his letter. When being led by the Spirit of Jesus, there comes a glorious freedom. There is no required obedience to any mechanical set of religious laws. We are privileged to live with and be guided by the fruit of the Spirit, the center of which s love. Against such there is no law.

> That love of God, in Jesus known,
> transfigures every thought and deed;
> The love we show ourselves, be shown
> in friendship to our neighbors' need.
>
> If love be all we need to know
> in earth beneath or heaven above,
>
> Enlist us, Lord, while here below,
> as learners in your school of love.[8]

---

[7] Barry L. Callen, *The Prayer of Holiness-Hungry People*.
[8] Lyrics by Timothy Dudley-Smith.

A Call To Action

A proper Christian prayer is: "Thank you, Lord, for your great love shown to us. Thank you for pouring your love into us so that we can live our lives by knowing and sharing it. We confess, however, that the lack of advance rules for behavior is sometimes hard to deal with. Please keep your loving Spirit close so that we will be able to determine what you would have us do as each new circumstance presents itself."

Here's are sure guidelines as we go. "Always abound in the work of the Lord" (1 Cor. 15:58). "Trust in Him at all times" (Ps. 62:8). "Never lose hope" (Lam. 3:25-26; Isa. 26:4). Love is adaptive to every present need, although it can be misused as a license for doing whatever we wish, trying to avoid accountability or please some religious authority. We so need the guidance of God's Spirit in all this! We need to be made holy as God is holy. Only as the Spirit lives within, controlling attitudes and actions, can the law of love be evidenced as it should.

The ongoing life of the church, through all its difficult ups and downs, is managed well only by the living and loving Spirit of God. Church life can have a lovely perfume (2 Cor. 2:15) and be an attractive letter to the world, but only when infused by the living Christ himself.

> That blessed law of Thine,
> Jesus, to me impart;
> The Spirit's law of life divine,
> O write it in my heart!
> Implant it deep within,
> Whence it may ne'er remove,
> The law of liberty from sin,
> The perfect law of love.[9]

---

[9] Charles Wesley, "The Thing My Lord Doth Hate."

Making Room For Others

Christian holiness involves recognizing the worth of all persons and risking oneself lovingly on their behalf. It's being so aware of the adequacy of the grace of God that we dare to allow God's graciousness to be present with us and flowing through us, even in our most awkward and frustrating human relationships. We must be holy dreamers, called to have transformational visions on behalf of broken communities and disadvantaged individuals. We must look beyond who people presently are to who they are intended to be and yet can be through God's welcoming grace. The love of God makes room for all, awkward as that sometimes can be.

Holiness is Welcoming and Loving the Unholy.
Christian Holiness is . . . Putting Oneself on the Altar.
Genesis 1; Galatians 2

Christian holiness is possible only because of the descent of God in Christ to our human plane so that we sinful humans can rise to a reuniting relationship with God through the Spirit of Christ. We can love because God first loved. God has made room for us, and now we must do the same for others. "Joy to the world, the Lord has come. . . Let every heart *prepare him room*."[1]

Hospitality is a way of describing the will of a Christian believer to keep wide open to God's ongoing revelation, spiritual-growth windows to life, and avenues of service to others. Reaching graciously and listening carefully are essential exercises of being truly Christian. To be *holy* is to be *hospitable*. To be one with God is necessarily to be in tune with God's presence, gifts, people, and creation, loving and caring for them in all always possible.

How frequently the opposite is the case. One of Martin Luther King's trademark lines came from the prophet Amos. King would clinch the power of an oration by proclaiming, "Let justice roll down like waters, and righteousness like an ever-flowing stream" (Amos 5:24). We now live in a society schooled in the belief that we are accountable to no one except ourselves—what's right is what seems right to us. Who are others to judge me? We want to be left alone to live our lives as we see fit, according to our own rules, regardless of what happens to others. This is a dangerously crooked individualism, the opposite of God's intended order.

God is the Present Host. With the baptism of Jesus, his disciples began to emerge and understand increasingly who he really was, what he came to do, and thus who they were to be as part of his ongoing mission. Jesus was a full human being and also the long-awaited Messiah. He was the greatest of all paradoxes, being simultaneously fully human and fully *God with us*.

Beginning on that baptism day at the Jordan River, Jesus redefined humanity and its understanding of divinity. Believers no longer could think of either without thinking of Jesus. God Almighty had become present in this young Jew from Nazareth. God is not distant and unloving, not with the Son so present with us and so self-

---

[1] Words by Isaac Watts, see Psalm 98.

giving for us. The Host of Heaven is with us and welcoming all to the table of saving and sanctifying grace!

According to Psalm 29, what we cannot do for ourselves God is able and anxious to do for us. We must hear the voice of the LORD thundering over the waters, appearing in holy splendor and majesty. We must ascribe to the LORD the honor due his name. God creates out of chaos and pain and rides triumphant even on the floods. We are invited to ride with him and rescue some who otherwise would be lost. We have been welcomed and now must be welcomers.

No matter how many negative scenes surrounded the birth and crucifixion of Jesus, there was one marvelous fact that rose above them all. The angels were singing "Glory to God!" God came to form a chosen people, a holy people, loving examples of the arriving reign of God. Therefore, let each of us humbly pray: "Include me among the chosen, Lord, and help me act in ways that fit my being one of your chosen creators of a new day. Make me holy as you are holy in ways that reach to the lost as you have reached to me."

God is a generous and gracious host. Israel was a stranger, an alien, a people with no home, wholly undeserving when God chose them, called them, and granted them an identity and future. Having been powerless sojourners in a foreign land (Deut. 10:19), they were welcomed by God and then called to welcome other strangers (Ex. 23:9). To be one with this most gracious God, Christians must risk keeping the welcome mat out and well-used to the glory of God (Rom. 15:7).

Jesus promised that welcoming the stranger, feeding the hungry, and visiting the sick and imprisoned would be counted as personal kindness to the Master himself (Matt. 25:35–45). My wife has heard this call and pleases the Master by serving several days each week at our local church pantry. She relates lovingly to hundreds of the disadvantaged who come through the doors for food and often minutes of human warmth and caring. She and I, through Horizon international, help serve thousands of orphaned children in five African nations. Such a local pantry and world mission are good places to meet and please Jesus!

Eagerly Welcoming People. Whatever the cost, Jesus people are called to build faith communities of radical grace and extravagant welcome. This is in sharp contrast to what many churches have been, exclusive communities defined more by detesting sin than loving sinners. The gracious hosting to be inspired by Christian holiness can be expensive, hard on facilities, harsh on treasured traditions of what we've always thought right and proper in God's house. No matter. It cost Jesus his life.

Christian holiness is not one life characteristic among others but the overarching quality, the source and sum of all virtues. It avoids injury to the neighbor and actively opens doors of hope to strangers in need. It dares to pioneer paths to God and keeps singing humbly, "Just as I Am, Without one Plea, But that Thy Blood was Shed for Me."[2] Despite our own inner negatives, when God calls, we are to respond, "I come, I come!" We eagerly welcome rather than nervously fear the cleansing work of God or the impact strangers may have on our religious establishments if we dare to let them inside.

Holiness without hospitality is empty and false. God's saints are to be open to the welcoming voice of the Spirit. They will make room for fellow believers, different or not, and even be anxious for friendship with and service to those still outside the faith community, hostile or not. To live in God's house is to breathe the Spirit's air and thus be involved in the Spirit's life and mission. A congregation is to anticipate the sensitivities of "outsiders." Each fellowship has a distinctive culture not always easy to join comfortably.

A recent study of hundreds of church visitors who didn't return for a second time was anything but encouraging. The church wasn't rude, not at all, just thoughtless about little things like signs, seating, greeters, etc.[3] By contrast in my own experience, the Gethsemane monastery in Kentucky maintains a gracious ministry of welcoming spiritual retreatants. My room and meals always have been ready, clean and nourishing, signs made with times and rules simple and clear. While they don't know me, never have I felt like an outsider because I'm a Protestant. They gladly accept donations but never ask for money. They require little and offer much. They are quiet

---

[2] Tender words of divine invitation and human response by Charlotte Elliott.
[3] See Thom S. Ranier, *Becoming a Welcoming Church*.

and prayerful agents of Jesus, making community participation easy and attractive.

Exploring The Biblical Text

John 15:1-17. Jesus makes clear that the only workable future rests on our being strong, open, welcoming, and connecting, instruments of healing and community-building. No branch can bear fruit by itself. Our Lord is the true vine, the source of life for all the branches. We are to abide in him and live by his love. We are to love one another as he has loved us. There are no exclusions—love all those loved by God.

We must keep this hard lesson in mind. Jesus was born in the poorest of settings because there was no place for him otherwise (Lk. 2:7). No favors were extended to the holy one of God. Nor should his holy children expect otherwise for themselves. The faithful go where they can and are faithful there as best they can. The angels are watching and, despite all, joyous songs will be heard.

An All-Bible Emphasis. In many biblical texts one finds God welcoming the sinner and God's people being called to do the same. Jesus was found in places and with people not normally judged acceptable by the mainstream Judaism of the time. He suffered the consequences, and also revealed the gracious heart of God.

The Jews of old were told this. "The alien who resides with you shall be to you as the native-born among you; you shall love the alien as yourself, for you were aliens in the land of Egypt" (Lev. 19:34). Jesus added this instruction. "But when you give a banquet, invite the poor, the crippled, the lame, and the blind. And you will be blessed because they cannot repay you, for you will be repaid at the resurrection of the righteous" (Lk. 14:13-14).

ENRICHING OUR UNDERSTANDING

God's Preference for the Poor. One of the more important themes of contemporary theology is the understanding that God has a "preferential option for the poor." I remember when the insistence on "plain dress" was central to the Holiness Movement's sense of integrity. We dressed down so we could live humbly, frugally, and the poor would not feel uncomfortable in our midst. Modesty was key to mission.[4] Mission to the poor was a prominent feature of the callings of the holiness people.

Gustavo Gutierrez's groundbreaking *A Theology of Liberation* helped chart a new course for the church in modern times, although hardly new to God. Extreme poverty and systemic injustice is where one tends to find Christ's presence most readily. Yes, we are saved by God's grace despite being wholly undeserving. Likewise, those souls who suffer greatly for no fault of their own appear to tug most strongly on God's loving heart. He passes the doors of the wealthy and invites the destitute to banquets of food, grace, and hope.

Here's the statement of a famous Christian theologian once a Nazi soldier against his will: "God is not on the side of the mighty as the 'Almighty'—God is on the side of the weak as the liberator in solidarity with them. In this godless world of violence, God's weakness has a revolutionary effect. 'He has brought down the powerful from their thrones and lifted up the lowly' (Lk. 1:52)."[5]

True Family Offered. The world is full of refugees, orphans, and other struggling persons. People don't feel accepted, don't belong, are disconnected and therefore experiencing life as aliens and strangers. Biblical revelation is not intended as more condemnation of those already suffering, but as love extended and true family offered.[6] One holiness body from its beginning committed itself to freedom of the Spirit in worship, of slaves from masters, and of church pews from rental fees that favored the rich.[7]

The fact is that once we all were far off before Christ came and proclaimed peace, and now we all have equal access to the Father through the Spirit (Eph. 2:17-22). The lyrics of Bill and Gloria Gaither state a spiritual reality longed for by many who otherwise are orphaned souls in this troubled world:

> I'm so glad I'm a part of the family of God,
> I've been washed in the fountain, cleansed by His blood,

---

[4] Donald W. Dayton, in the *Wesleyan Theological Journal*, 1991.
[5] Jürgen Moltmann, *The Living God and the Fullness of Life*.
[6] Barry L. Callen, *Authentic Spirituality*.
[7] The Free Methodist Church of North America.

Joint heirs with Jesus as we travel this sod,
For I'm part of the family, the family of God.

Who Is a Racist? Most of us would answer, "Them but not me!" A recent study questions our quick denial. It's not easy to escape participating in social stratification that's standard in one's culture. More than 150 years after the 13th Amendment abolished slavery in the United States, most U. S. adults today say the legacy of slavery continues to have an impact on the position of Black people in American society. When I was a kid it was called the "pecking order." Even in church life there is a division between the powers and perks of clergy and laity, the superiority of my denomination or nation or skin color over yours, the usually unspoken preference for "people like us."

Our larger social scene may not feature the sharp divisions like the caste system of India or the recent apartheid system of South Africa, but there still are traditional social classes that quietly privilege some over others. Life today still is subtly defined by a hierarchy of human social divisions.[8] We still build walls to keep out the unwanted. Jesus says, "Let them in!"

A Call To Action

Our generation has known too little of the life-giving character of Christian hospitality. One contemporary Christian woman combines rich biblical and historical research with extensive exposure to contemporary Christian communities like the Catholic Worker, L'Abri Fellowship, L'Arche, Jubilee Partners, and The Open Door. Her resulting book shows how understanding the key features of hospitality in action can better equip faithful Christians to carry out the practical call of the gospel of Christ.[9]

Differing though we may be in many ways, love links us all who belong to Christ and comprise his church. We are called to champion that blessed togetherness and then reach out to welcome others.

Blest be the tie that binds
Our hearts in Christian love,

---

[8] Isabel Wilkerson, *Caste*.
[9] Christine D. Pohl, *Making Room*.

> The fellowship of kindred minds
> Is like to that above.[10]

Christian holiness functions as active openness to each other and especially to the most isolated humans in need of fellowship and the love of Christ. The people of ancient Israel understood themselves as strangers and sojourners with responsibility to care for the strangers in their midst. Again, Jesus promised that welcoming the stranger, feeding the hungry, and visiting the sick and imprisoned would be counted as personal kindness to the Master himself (Matt. 25:35-45).

Any who wish to be holy in a Christian sense, and thus to be the true church of Christ, must honor words such as these:

> Let us build a house
> where love can dwell,
> and all can safely live;
> A place where saints and children tell
> how hearts learn to forgive.
>
> Built of hopes and dreams and visions,
> rock of faith and vault of grace;
> Here the love of Christ shall end divisions.
>
> All are welcome, all are welcome,
> all are welcome in this place.[11]

---

[10] Lyrics by John Fawcett.
[11] Lyrics by Marty Haugen.

Assuring a Holy Church

While none of us knows the future, there are some important guidelines to follow as we, God's church, walk together into the unknown. We are wise to follow these guidelines and remember that it's *God's* church, not ours. Its integrity is assured only by the Spirit's constant presence and guiding and enabling power. Its mission effectiveness depends on receiving and using the gifts of the Spirit that are intended for the good of the whole body. A holy church is one infused, gifted, guided, and sent into the world by the Spirit.

Being a Holy Church of God. Christian Holiness is . . . Enriching the Body of Believers. Luke 4:16-30; 1 Corinthians 12:1-11

Of course this is a different day. Even so, the "last days" have been every day since the time of Jesus. Rather than the church despairing because of new challenges, it's time to relish new opportunities, to be a holy church, one ready for the Lord's return in large part by being busy with the Lord's urgent work in the meantime. While we don't know the Lord's calendar, we do know our present commission to be a "holy" church serving a broken world. The most ancient and still common creed of Christianity, then, puts it this way:

> I believe in the Holy Spirit,
> the holy catholic church,
> the communion of saints,
> the forgiveness of sins,
> the resurrection of the body,
> and life everlasting.

What constitutes a *holy* church? Key characteristics are:

- Belief in the Holy Spirit who is welcomed to constitute and infuse all of church life;

- Commitment to being "catholic" by living with a vision that actively welcomes the whole body of Christ worldwide;

- Participating in active relationship (communion) with the larger body, risking the diversity as an avenue of enrichment;

- Reaching to the lost, knowing forgiveness for yesterday's wrongs, and assured of God's promised future.

Always a New Day. A holy church honors God's "now" time. After all, the Spirit of Jesus has come! Individuals must yield to divine holiness, and so must the church in its many expressions, institutions, and mission strategies. The vision of a holy church sees the whole body of believers united in loving mission, rejoicing together in God's good grace and assured of God's good future.

Inspired Christian messengers in our new time are needed to blow the holy-church trumpets. God's time still, as always, is *now*! To be a truly holy people, believers must de-emphasize speculation about supposed knowledge of "end times" and highlight the constant importance of mission in the present through the transforming power of God's Spirit.[1]

There is need to repudiate unfortunate preoccupations that have burdened many generations. Christians must counter the temptation to claim absolute finality for passing church institutions, theological systems, and the supposed power of human reason to know and "prove" the truth to public satisfaction. Authentic Christianity requires faith, grace, and inner transformation. A holy church knows that room must be left for mystery, diversity, and continuing spiritual growth. Dynamic new life in God's Spirit always is to be the central reality.

Members of the first-century Corinthian congregation were dividing into factions based on preferred spiritual teachers, each group claiming superior status. Paul explains to them that a variety of spiritual gifts are given by God's Spirit "for the common good" and not personal prominence. No spiritual gift should be used to disrupt the fellowship for one's own benefit.

There's been an unfortunate Protestant emphasis on the "invisible" church, the true church supposedly being what we can't see beneath its maze of human structures, practices, and failures. This emphasis lowers the vision of God's intention for the church, justifying rampant denominationalism and encouraging a splintering individualism among believers. The goal of Christian faith is to be the holy church that openly reflects the present life of God so that the world *can see* it and be drawn to it.

The Higher Vision. The biblical call is for believers to be *"filled with the Spirit"* (Eph. 5:18b) and then live and serve peaceably together as God's holy people. Here's the doctrinal logic drawn from two holiness hymns:

> The soul longs for being "fully saved."
> How? By being filled with God's Spirit.
> Such filling brings a "purification" that makes one "whole."
> This wholeness brings a "single eye," rendering one
> "perfect" and fully acceptable in God's sight.

---

[1] See Barry L. Callen, *Faithful in the Meantime*.

> This perfection is possible because it's God's will to "sanctify."
> Being filled with "perfect love" makes one God's very own,
> allowing the humble believer to be "ever all Thine own."
> The result is a vibrant and authentic Christian witness, namely,
> "Let Thy glory in me shine, Let Thy fire within me glow."[2]
>
> The experience of "perfectness" creates
> a "sweet bond" among believers, a "fellowship so precious,"
> which in turn "unites us all in Jesus"
> with a "union heaven gave us."[3]

The holy children of a holy God find spiritual community with each other despite their diversity. The God-given unity in the Spirit enables an authentic witness to the life-transforming and church-forming love of God.

The church of Jesus is to embody "the highest vision of Christian unity, genuine openness coupled with true piety, sturdy beliefs without stultifying dogmas."[4] The church must hold in balance its affirmations and continuing questions. Now is the appointed time to start "seeing" the church again—and then actually *being* the church instead of merely *going* to church. Effective evangelism requires moving from good talking about the church to giving public evidence of the actual presence of its intended holiness and unity.

No church group has a corner on truth. Authority lies in biblical revelation and apostolic teachings as ministered to us by God's Holy Spirit. Going back to the right past, and doing it in community with each other, is necessary to get to the right future. It's a holy quest, a whole-church quest to encounter the God who always is seeking to encounter us.

Walking Future Paths. Jesus told his disciples to wait and receive the Spirit's baptism before proceeding with their world mission (Acts 1:4-5). Christian faith is a Spirit experience of holy newness experienced in community. Believers in Christ are to be both *free* in the Spirit and mutually *accountable* to each other in the Spirit

---

[2] Lyrics of *"Fill Me with Thy Spirit, Lord"* by Daniel S. Warner.
[3] Daniel S. Warner, "The Bond of Perfectness."
[4] Robert A. Nicholson, in Barry L. Callen, *Faith, Learning, and Life.*

community. Real spiritual life is not in passing church institutions. It's in being the people of God by receiving together the gifting and serving wisdom and power of the Spirit.

The church is to be God's holy sanctuary. We are to think *body*, witnessing well to the world because we are evidencing a corporate holiness by being the obvious community of Jesus. Being renewed in the Spirit requires a holiness that inspires and gladly embraces "a true rainbow of humanity where color, tribe, race, and culture are all featured—but never allowed to be a divisive factor."[5]

It's in this communal embracing that the Bible is read best. The spiritually mature Christian loves the Bible and readily studies it *in community*. The holy ones know their limitations and need the wisdom of the whole body of Christ. We are to be present together in the church as a way of increasing our openness to the body's Spirit and wisdom.

As believers walk future mission paths together, "perhaps Western culture is nearing the point where the Christian faith can be successfully re-introduced."[6] If so, holiness experienced individually and matured in community will lie at the center of the reintroduction. This has been true of the great Christian revivals over the centuries under various names but always in the "holy river of God."[7]

Exploring The Biblical Text

Luke 4:16-30. Jesus came to his hometown, spoke, was rejected, but in the process shared valuable guidelines for how to be his people. Those gathered in that Nazareth synagogue were astonished at what he said. They were good Jews shocked when he countered their usual ways of worshipping God. He taught as one with authority, making clear that the Word of God is in charge of worship life.

Divine proclamation is always to be on center stage in the church. The presence of God's Spirit is to be sought and relied on to interpret the Father's ultimate wisdom. The church must be organized so that it's capable of and willing to alter the normal flow of things when human need calls and the Spirit speaks. There must be room

---

[5] Hubert P. Harriman and Barry L. Callen, *Color Me Holy*.

[6] Howard A. Snyder, *The Radical Wesley & Patterns of Church Renewal*.

[7] Barry L. Callen, ed., *The Holy River of God*.

provided for the impulses of the Spirit. It's God's church, after all, not ours.

1 Corinthians 12:1-11. Religious "institutionalism" is a threat to true Christian salvation and mission. It's a human replacement for the pure grace of the saving God. We humans often try working our way to heaven, earning our salvation, keeping it for ourselves and our kind, and formalizing it in controlling structures and standards. God already has opened the door of divine grace to all people, most being unlike us in many ways. There is a variety of gifts but only one Spirit. We humans tend to resist, opting to choose our spiritual brothers and sisters according to selfish preferences. Such resistance is so unlike Jesus. It's Christianity gone wrong. Going right is when "all are activated by one and the same Spirit" (12:11).

Enriching Our Understanding

Radical, Visible, and Charismatic. John Wesley was a "radical" Christian. Christian radicality insists that, at all costs, the church must be a visible community that takes seriously the demands of discipleship. With his emphasis on the Holy Spirit, Wesley's faith was also "charismatic." Early Methodism was above all a movement of spiritual renewal. It was a mass movement of people coming to know the power of God and of genuine Christian community in their daily lives. "Thou Who almighty art, now rule in every heart, and ne'er from us depart, Spirit of Power!"[8]

The Church, A Place of "Mystery"! "The church must show the world that the kingdom of God has come. There must be something about the church that is beyond culture, nationality, race, class, and education. The church falls when she becomes too strongly tied to a particular culture. That is why I oppose the creation of white churches or black churches. There is nothing mysterious about a church made of people who look alike and act alike. Such a church says nothing very significant to the world, especially if the world feels unwelcome there. There must be something in the church that

---

[8] Charles Wesley, "Come, Thou Almighty King."

cannot be explained except by the fact that *God lives in his people.*"⁹ The crucial difference lies in the mystery of divine grace and the obvious presence in the church of the holiness of God forming a people who reflect that holiness in their attitudes and actions. The result is a people not known otherwise by the world.

Holiness to be a Corporate Reality. One insightful sister shares this. "While I have always defined the image of God in *relational* terms, I haven't always understood it in *communal* terms. We are, *as a community*, holy people. We together are the holy, although in some ways still the broken body of Christ. When one part suffers, all suffer. When one part rejoices, all rejoice. We Jesus people are to live interdependently, relying on the strengths of each other. This is the meaning of solidarity so central to the holiness tradition. This is the true community which God calls the church to be. Even in our weakness, together we can be strong, even holy."[10]

God's call to holy community is basic to all biblical revelation. It began with the calling Abraham, not merely as an individual but as the beginning of a people of God that would transcend time, national boundaries, and racial discriminations. "The call is not just to individuals but to form, be, and act like a people, a human community in solidarity internally and with God, a people in covenant with God, so closely connected that their actual way of life is shaped more by God's character than by the nations and cultures all around."[11] The church is "a chosen race, a royal priesthood, a holy nation" (1 Pet. 2:9). Holiness is central to its very nature and integrity. The church's way of life is to be shaped by God's character, holy love.

A Call To Action

For the church to be formed by and oriented around the presence and work of the Spirit of God is not necessarily to be mired in subjectivism or committed to individualism in church life. Spirit orientation is the conscious determination of Christian believers to be

---

[9] Samuel G. Hines, in Barry Callen, *The Wisdom of the Saints*.
[10] Diane Leclerc, in Barry Callen and Don Thorsen, *Heart & Life*.
[11] Howard A. Snyder, in Mannoia and Thorsen, *The Holiness Manifesto*.

free of artificial and forced structures of belief and church life and, conversely, to be committed to spiritual reality, serious discipleship, credible covenant community, and social mission.[12]

Are you free and committed in these dramatic ways? If not, will you dare to become so now? God's people are his children over all the earth, living and now dead, experiencing "eternal life" because of their intimate relationship with the Spirit of Jesus Christ. They are on a mission of the Spirit of love and filled with and propelled by these wonderful truths:

> The church's one foundation
> is Jesus Christ, her Lord;
> She is his new creation
> by water and the Word.
>
> From heav'n he came and sought her
> to be his holy bride;
> With his own blood he bought her,
> and for her life he died.[13]

---

[12] Barry L. Callen, *Radical Christianity*.
[13] Lyrics by S. J. Stone.

A United Christ Community

A major movement in the worldwide Christian community in recent generations has been the "ecumenical" one. It has sought an answer to this question. How can the church of Jesus solve its problem of severe dividedness for the sake of a more effective witness to the world? Creedal and structural unification attempts have been many, and mostly have succeeded only partially at best. Christian holiness, unity "in the Spirit," is one approach that can enable what the church so needs. Only the love of God can bind our hearts together and send us out on common mission. The call to holiness is also the call to togetherness in love. It's the Jesus way that transcends a mere realigning of denominational bureaucracies. It requires a reforming of human hearts.

The Unity of the Church was a Key Concern of Jesus.
Christian Holiness is . . . Reaching for Partnerships.
John 17; Ephesians 2:11-22; Colossians 3:14

It happened only a few generations after first being launched as the new family of the resurrected Jesus. Much of the young church evolved into an institutionalized power structure that mirrored the dominant Roman Empire. Centuries later in the Western world, protesting disciples (Protestants) bolted the institutional grip of the Roman Catholic Church. Soon, however, they found themselves organized into competitive "denominations" often allied with various national governments. Such divisive trends also were experienced in much of the Eastern world.

The one faith in Jesus Christ now has many expressions and structural commitments, often subtly competitive and even allied with secular bodies. There are numerous national councils of churches and a formalized World Council of Churches. The integrity of the church must be restored. God intends a united body of Christ, proclaiming the Master with one voice and without compromise. The goal will not be reached easily.

The World Council seeks to function "as an instrument to assist its member bodies bear witness together to their common allegiance to Jesus Christ, search for the unity Christ wills for his church, and cooperate in matters that require common statements and actions." Many relational gains have been enabled through this international and inter-denominational organization, although many Christian bodies don't cooperate as members. They fear an underlying agenda of structuring one world church, possibly dominated by Rome, and/or an affirming of stances on political, doctrinal, or moral issues considered unacceptably "liberal."

True Christian preaching is "the sharing of the words of Christ and the mediation of his presence through the anointing of his indwelling Spirit, so that hearers are aroused to respond to the call to be *like Christ in holiness*."[1] God's intention surely is such a holy proclamation coming from a body of disciples who have become holy themselves by the gracious action of the Spirit of Christ. This intention has proven illusive, in part because the church remains stubbornly divided.

---

[1] James Earl Massey, in Mannoia and Thorsen, *The Holiness Manifesto*.

The Unfinished Quest. The twentieth was the "ecumenical" century in search of solutions to the prevailing dividedness of the body of Christ. A series of Christian diplomats sought to further the unifying cause. The basic problem persists. The New Testament's suggested solution is restored interpersonal relationships marked by the holiness of Christian hearts that yearn to be together for Christ's sake. Believers are to know themselves as the one family of Christ by the Spirit's action on behalf of a common mission.

To be "holy" is to move beyond the question "What must I do to be saved?" to the equally crucial question, "What must I be and do now that I am saved?" One key answer to the second question is to begin doing as Jesus prayed (Jn. 17), reaching for partnership and fellowship with all followers of the Master so that believers can be truly *together* on mission for the Father through the Spirit.

Believers are "to seek first the kingdom of God and his righteousness" (Matt. 6:33). Kingdom loyalties are to be put ahead of all others. Recognition must be given to the likelihood that the Spirit of God is at work in traditions of the Christian faith other than our own. Such a holy humility is key to Christian unity. Whatever our differences, we who belong to Christ belong to each other and need each other. We are to expect enrichment and not threat from the diversity of belief and practice we find in other believers.

Restored Relationships. An important focus of Christian holiness is becoming dedicated to restored relationships within the body of Christ. Avoided must be the historic dilemma of judging others by a strict set of creedal and behavioral expectations that we and "our church" prefer. John Wesley's famous phrase "perfect love" should be thought of as the mature spiritual life centered in a truly restored relationship to God that seeks to find restoration with all other believers.

"Sanctification" is a set-apartness *for God* that leans in the direction of the reestablishment of right relationships *with each other*. The unity needed and possible among believers comes through the dynamic of the Spirit's love. Love is the supreme gift given to the church. It's to supersede all forms of spiritual individualism and the exclusive dominance of particular church traditions. Such traditions have their ways of undermining church life and mission by obstructing the free flow of the work of the Spirit.

Spiritual gifts are given to the church by the Spirit of Christ for the purpose of building up the body *in unity* and *for mission* (Eph. 4:11–12). The God who is *over* and *for* us (God the Father and Son) now is available to be *in* and *through* us (God the Spirit). This holy presence brings a unity among otherwise quite diverse Christian believers. It's this Spirit unity that enables effective witness of the church to the world. Holy believers are intentionally partner believers on joint mission.

While Christian unity is a gift from God through the Spirit, it's realized only as Christians open themselves to community with all other believers. Unity may be divinely given, but "our experience of it must be gained. Belonging to Jesus Christ makes every believer belong to all other believers."[2] True church unity is "where the diverse members of the body of Christ are aware of and appreciate their essential relatedness to each other, where they love one another with the kind of love with which they have been loved."[3]

This restorative love is a holy gift of the Spirit of love. It can be employed well only if church bodies don't retreat within themselves out of presumed self-protection, fearing "contamination" by the differing beliefs and practices of other Christian believers. The potential of fulfilling the prayer of Jesus (Jn. 17) is destroyed when believers refuse to move openly and creatively among other members of the larger body.

Finding the Middle Ground. Christians must seek to be properly *convictional* without being prematurely and narrowly *creedal*. All believers and their church bodies are, or at least should be in process and on pilgrimage. Humility should mark all persons graciously restored by a holy God to their intended holiness of thinking and acting. Biblical truth may be definite and final, but our human understanding and expressions of it are necessarily partial and to be growing. We do that best *together*.

---

[2] James Earl Massey, *Concerning Christian Unity*.
[3] Clark Williamson, *A Guest in the House of Israel*.

How do believers with diverse understandings of divine revelation avoid straying from God's intentions and hurtfully dividing from each other in the process? Those who worship the Father are instructed to do so "in spirit and in truth" (Jn. 4:23-24), always in close relation to "the Spirit of truth" (Jn. 14:17, 15:26, 16:13). Whatever the church's organizational patterns, its integrity depends a common relationship to God's Spirit.

Beyond all theological expressions, church practices, and beloved religious structures, Jesus is *the truth* (14:6), and he is conveyed to us best *by his Spirit*. Faith should be placed more in the divine Person than in any human proposition we formulate about Jesus or structures we create in his name. Our unity as believers is dependent on relating to the Spirit of Jesus and being enriched by various streams of holiness understanding present in the larger body of Christ. "In so doing, we may end up finding ways to better unite and cooperate in our common goals of uplifting God, who is holy, and becoming more like God in all dimensions of life."[4]

Organizational variety appears inevitable since the church is comprised of believers from widely differing backgrounds and understandings of the faith and its implementations in differing cultures. Even so, the goal of Christian unity is to present to the world a loving church that obviously hears and follows one Spirit in the midst of all its diversity, and thus can love each other and serve together regardless of the differences. Christian holiness truly experienced and shared is the only viable way ahead.

Believers in Jesus must find ways to be "strengthened in our inner beings" by Christ dwelling within through the power of his Spirit (Eph. 3:16-17). This, however, is hardly a private business. God's work is active within "us" and can accomplish even more than "we" can imagine (vs. 18). We comprehend and serve best "with all the saints." To God be glory "in the church" (vs. 21), in Christ and his Spirit, and in fellowship with all the faithful. We learn of God best in the community of God's people and then serve God best *together* in the world.

---

[4] Kevin Mannoia and Don Thorsen, eds., *The Holiness Manifesto*.

Exploring The Biblical Text

John 17. What could be of more concern to the church of Jesus than what Jesus asks the Father on its behalf? He seeks the same oneness among today's church members as exists always between Father and Son. This oneness is holiness, defined as believers having in themselves "the joy of Christ made complete" (Jn. 17:13). If this joy is experienced in the fellowship of Jesus, the church will become united in a way that will help the world know that the Jesus people are more than another religious body of frail humans. This call to shared holiness, and thus Christian unity, comes with a promise. "Finally, brothers and sisters, rejoice! Strive for full restoration, encourage one another, be of one mind, live in peace, and the God of love and peace will be with you" (2 Cor. 13:11).

Ephesians 2:11-22. Paul identifies something as "above all." What is it? We believers must "clothe ourselves with love, which binds everything together in perfect harmony" (Col. 3:14). To be "holy" is to enable unity to reign in the body of Christ by allowing "the peace of Christ to rule in your hearts" (Col. 3:15). Once we all were outsiders, aliens, strangers to the covenant of promise. But Christ has broken down the dividing wall and hostility between outsiders and insiders in order to reconcile everyone to God in one body through the cross. Now there are no aliens since all have equal access to God and his one household, which is the Lord's "holy temple." Thank God for the one holy church! May Christians come to function beyond the usual walls of denominationalism, thinking of each church group as an "evangelical order of witness and worship, discipline and nurture" within "an encompassing environment of catholicity."[5]

Enriching Our Understanding

Patterns of Partnership. Denominated bodies of Christians can be effective representatives of God's Spirit if they are not honored as ends in themselves and they function cooperatively in patterns

---

[5] Albert Outler, in *The Wesleyan Theological Heritage*, Oden and Longden, eds.

of partnership with the whole body of believers. All should function as "movements" seeking to facilitate the health of the whole church. Christian unity is both a gift of God and the achievement of those committed to its realization. The diamond of Christian truth has many facets. Difference is a negative only it deviates from the biblical revelation that is to form the church in all its expressions.[6]

The Need Is Radical Reconciliation. Uniformity of doctrine or coming together under one form of church government cannot produce Christian unity. The unity of the church emerges only through the organic unity of the people who are intentionally constituted spiritually as the body of Christ. Christ unites through his Spirit. In our attempt to achieve organizational unity through mergers, councils, and conclaves, we too often neglect the need for the radical action of reconciliation, a reconciliation grounded in our total love for God and our mutual love for each other. Jesus said that our most important tool for evangelism would be our love for each other (Jn. 13:34–35).[7]

John Wesley advocated a "catholic spirit." "Although a difference in opinions or modes of worship may prevent an entire external union, yet need it prevent our union in affection? Though we can't think alike, may we not love alike? May we not be of one heart, though we are not of one opinion? Without all doubt we may. Herein all the children of God may unite, notwithstanding the smaller differences."[8]

A Call To Action

Being "holy" by full life commitment to the Spirit of Jesus allows a loving openness "in the Spirt" to flow toward all sisters and brothers in the faith. Have you done this? Will you do this? The Spirit of holiness and oneness is calling you to be an agent of Christian unity! Can you envision this? Do you long to be part of it? Such Christian unity can't happen on mere human terms. You and I first must be

---

[6] Barry Callen and James North, *Coming Together in Christ*.
[7] Samuel G. Hines, *Beyond Rhetoric*.
[8] Howard A. Snyder, *The Radical Wesley*. See John Wesley's sermon titled "Catholic Spirit."

made holy by love reigning in our hearts, on the way to the body itself becoming holy and thus more attractive to the lost world.

May your heart start singing and your life start reflecting these hymn words: "How sweet this bond of perfectness, The wondrous love of Jesus, A pure foretaste of heaven's bliss, *O fellowship so precious*!"[9] The unity goal is not *uniformity* but *reconciliation* in the midst of diversity, love reigning among disciples of Jesus as together they are committed to spreading the good news of Jesus Christ.

> Diverse in culture, nation, race,
> We come together by Your grace.
> God, let us be a meeting ground,
> Let us be a table spread with gifts
> of love and broken bread,
> Where all find welcome, grace attends,
> and enemies arise as friends.[10]

No geography should be allowed to separate Christians who find their true unity in the "high communion" of holy love that transcends their human diversities.

> In Christ there is no east or west,
> in him no south or north,
> but one great fellowship of love
> throughout the whole wide earth.
>
> In Christ shall true hearts ev'rywhere
> their high communion find.
> His service is the golden cord
> close binding humankind.[11]

---

[9] "The Bond of Perfectness" by Daniel S. Warner, based on Colossians 3:14.
[10] Lyrics by Ruth Duck.
[11] Lyrics by John Oxenham.

Heaven's Eventual Population

This could be the longest or shortest of all the chapters. Heaven is the greatest of our hopes and the one about which we know the least. We all talk about it although none of us has ever been there. Whatever, wherever, and whenever it will be, one thing is clear. It is the origin and home of holiness, the destiny of the holiness quest, and the indescribable realm of never-ending love and joy. Holiness, we're sure, is the ticket always honored at its door. The seeking Spirit of God covers the earth with redeeming love. The people who eventually go to heaven are all alike in at least one way. They are sinners who have received this love and placed their faith in the Lord Jesus Christ (Jn. 1:12; Acts 16:31; Rom. 10:9). What about those many loving seekers of truth who never even heard the name of Jesus? God will be the Judge.

Holiness is a Taste of Heaven Now. Christian Holiness is . . . Witnessing and Humbly Waiting. Isaiah 25:8-12; Romans 9:1-7

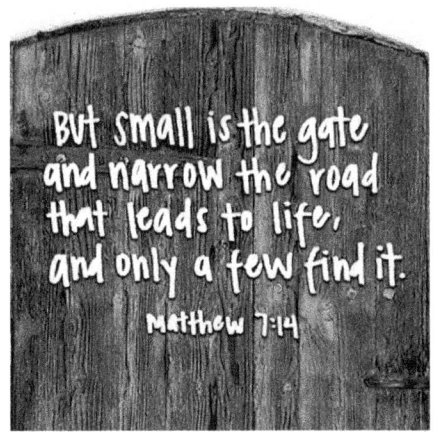

Heaven is the eventual destiny of true believers, persons reborn by the Spirit. At this point it's more hoped for than known. Since it's a vision of something so desirable, how do we get there? Jesus is the way, but the only way to heaven? He did say, "I am the way and the truth and the life. No one comes to the Father except through me" (Jn. 14:6). This exclusive claim appears to view the revelation of God in Jesus Christ as the unique, singular, and fully adequate truth path that must be followed if there is hope of eternal salvation.

A saving relationship with Jesus Christ is required to join heaven's population. Who will be there? All those who are set apart for God, chosen by God to be like him and with him forever. In this eternal "place," God will have swallowed death and wiped away the tears from all eyes (Isa. 25). God's election of Israel will be consummated, although "not all of Abraham's children are his descendants" (Rom. 9). People of all tribes, nations, and ethnicities will be there.

Restrictions to Heaven's Population? A question naturally arises. Doesn't the exclusive Jesus-only view unfairly limit heaven's population? After all, the majority of humanity has existed without ever hearing the Christian gospel. Are all non-Christian religious communities to be thought of as automatically excluded from heaven? Would that be just, the act of a merciful God? What is the proper Christian attitude toward non-Jesus people who nonetheless are serious about what they believe and how they live (holy in their own ways)? Does God's redeeming love transcend the walls of Christian churches and the frailty of ous theological thinking and evangelistic witnessing?

The Bible takes sin seriously and hardly encourages belief that everyone will accept God's love, although offered to all.[1] Nonetheless, Scripture also emphasizes the universal significance of Christ's atonement and "the ever-present Spirit who can foster transforming relationships with God anywhere and everywhere. The Spirit in-

---

[1] "Universalism" is an attractive idea--God loves all, will not fail, so all eventually will be saved. The problem is that humans have been given free-will, the ability and responsibility to choose, and our choices matter. Many choose against God.

spires hope in us, not only for our future but also for the future of the world and the ungodly whom God desires to justify (Rom. 15:13)."[2]

Biblically speaking, Jesus Christ is the only Mediator between God and humans. It also is said, however, that the activity of the loving Spirit of Christ pre-dates the sacrifice of Christ's atonement that occurred in relatively recent human history. Given the justice of God, this seems to offer hope for salvation beyond personal engagement with the historical Jesus event.

It's clearly possible to receive the mercy of God even when one's theology is incomplete, otherwise we all would be counted out. Surely, then, people can receive the gift of the Father's love without knowing exactly who the giver is or the name of the Son.

"Prevenient grace" is a very important biblical concept. It refers to the gracious and universal ministry of the Spirit.[3] God enables human faith response prior to any ability on our own to do so given our sinful condition. Therefore, the following affirmation is plausible, and I trust fully true. The Spirit of God is working on behalf of salvation wherever people are opening themselves to the loving ideals of Jesus and seeking holiness of heart and life as best they can understand and implement it in their life circumstances. The loving Spirit of God is present and honoring the holiness quest of all who are reaching in faith toward God.

Benefit *From* without Knowing *About*? A basic knowledge of God is universally available. Even so, apart from the grand expression of God's gracious saving activity in Jesus Christ, it's only partial knowledge at best. The cross that once appeared outside Jerusalem was planted in the heart of God before it ever was planted by the Romans. Its restorative love permeated the original creation and was the cause of Israel's Exodus.[4] By God's ever-present and loving grace, one surely can benefit from the work of God in Christ without

---

[2] Clark H. Pinnock, *Flame of Love*.

[3] On the possibility of the salvation of non-Christians as understood in the teachings of John Wesley, see Randy Maddox in his *Responsible Grace* and in the *Wesleyan Theological Journal* (27, 1992).

[4] See Barry L. Callen, *The Jagged Journey*.

direct awareness of the name Jesus or his historical life and sacrifice in the first century.

All human response to God, directly in Jesus Christ or through him indirectly, is possible only because of the universal presence and working of God's grace. The Christian claim is that this grace, always rooted in and best exemplified by the atoning work of Christ, always has been active in the universal ministry of Christ's Spirit, regardless of the level of human knowledge.

The Wesleyan-Holiness tradition of Christianity stresses the importance of human response to divine grace. It's open to but hesitates to embrace "universalism" (belief that all persons finally will be saved).[5] Instead, the belief is that all *can be* saved, although by choice likely *will not be*. Any claim to knowing precisely heaven's population, its eventual numbers, ethnicities, denominations, faith communities, and theological understandings, is not warranted. Making such judgments is "way above our pay grade" as mere humans. All are called to be holy and, by God's grace, surely all can be holy if they choose.

There are two errors clearly to be avoided. One is to assume dogmatically that all persons will be saved. The other is to say dogmatically that only a pre-selected few will be saved. Rather than stepping into the arrogant hole of these dogmatisms, we should focus on a humble acceptance of the amazing grace of God, spread the good news of Jesus Christ as far as possible, and leave to God a determination of the eventual population of heaven.

Exploring The Biblical Text

Isaiah 25:8-12. Heaven is less a known place and more a marvelous future circumstance resulting from God's most gracious actions. Already, reports the prophet Isaiah, God has done wonderful things. What will God yet do in the future? Swallow up death, wipe away tears, and abolish the pride of the evil-doers. Those first now will be the last then (Lk. 13:30). We know at least this much from Jesus himself. It's the *righteous* who will be ushered into eternal

---

[5] Consider Clark Pinnock's "hermeneutic of hopefulness" in his *A Wideness in God's Mercy*.

life (Matt. 25:46). There are many residences being prepared in that eternal realm for the holy faithful, and Jesus will come back and take them there to be with him personally forever (Jn. 14:2-4). There will be a new creation, although little about it is yet known, except that it will be everything we could possibly want!

Romans 9:1-7. God sanctifies us, sets us apart as authentic messengers of the gospel of Christ. "We misread the Bible if we believe that God sanctifies us only for our own betterment or eternal salvation. There is no such thing as sanctified selfishness."[6] Paul says, "I could wish that I myself were cursed and cut off from Christ for the sake of the people of Israel" (9:3). That attitude is evidence of sanctification, deep love for others because of Christ. It's to be holy as God is holy.

The great love of God reaches out to everyone. Who, then, will be in God's heaven? Potentially everyone since God's love covers all people, and all of Abraham's children are not his descendants (9:7). The word "potentially" is needed, however, because people have choices to make, and the choices have eternal consequences. We must leave to the final Judge what happens to those who never heard the story of God in Christ. The choice they face seems a little different.

At least one stark reality is clear regarding those who have heard the saving story of Jesus. They know that he prayed for the divine kingdom to come *on earth* now as a gracious foretaste of what one day will come *in heaven*. He asks the Father to "sanctify" his disciples for their present Christian mission, and this "holiness" comes with a warning. "Not everyone who says to Me, 'Lord, Lord,' shall enter the kingdom of Heaven" (Matt. 7:21). Faithfulness now, "doing the will of our Father in heaven," is prerequisite to later entrance into heaven. We don't earn salvation, certainly, but we who receive the grace of God surely will act lovingly out of its richness. If we do not, what was so sweet will sour within us.

---

[6] Diane Leclerc, *Discovering Christian Holiness*.

Enriching Our Understanding

Divine Grace Extends to All. The light of "prevenient" grace is a universal benefit of the meritorious death of Christ on the cross. God enables our ability to respond despite our sinfulness. There is a constant connection between the *Son of God* and the *Spirit of Christ* who is at work in every human heart in all times and places. This working of grace provides the universal possibility for salvation and holy living. It provides a way of understanding and affirming the essentials of the true religion of Jesus, even by people of other religious traditions.

With the help of God's undeserved grace, Christian holiness can *include* rather than *exclude* multiple ways of being "religious," ways that are acceptable to God.[7] Holiness is the adventure of going through life *with God* by the enabling grace and guidance of God's Spirit, and despite limited knowledge and imperfect life performance. It's accepting into our lives the reign of God and thereby becoming an active agent of the love of God for others. Whoever so accepts and becomes belongs to God, now and always.

Misguided Schemes of the Future. The ultimate future? The Bible provides divine foundations, impulses, intents, and assurances, but not calendars and grand political schemes with contemporary nametags. There are too many preachers with inflated confidence in their supposedly inspired biblical interpretations. They skate on very thin ice by building elaborate systems of future expectation and calling the end result "exactly what the Bible says."[8]

The purpose of Scripture is not to satisfy our curiosity about tomorrow but prepare us for today, to "provide training in righteousness so that we may be equipped for every good work" (2 Tim. 3:16-17). "If the Christian hope is reduced to the salvation of the soul in a heaven beyond death, it loses its power to renew life and change the world; it dies away into no more than a yearning for redemption from this world's veil of tears."[9]

---

[7] Philip R. Meadows, in Callen and Thorsen, *Heart & Life.*

[8] James Earl Massey, quoted in Barry Callen, *Heart of the Matter.*

[9] Jürgen Moltmann, *The Coming of God.*

Loving Instead of Being Defensive. David Bundy calls E. Stanley Jones "perhaps the best-known of the thousands of Anglo-Saxon missionaries active in India in modern times." In 1938 *Time* magazine called Jones "the world's greatest missionary evangelist." In India he experienced a major reorientation of his general theological stance. The change released this humble missionary to his unusually productive ministry. At first the theology of Jones had been neatly tied up with a blue ribbon and defensive. But he placed the securities of his faith on the altar and became free to explore, to appropriate any good, any truth found anywhere. This allowed him to *love* rather than *pity* India.[10] Our proclamations of Christ are to be both bold and humble.

A Call To Action

The world in which we minister in the name of Jesus is full of violence and death. Our role is to see and share the larger truth, which is that it all will be gone one day! Death will be dead. Injustice will be reversed. Meanwhile, the possibilities of the Father's life and love are to be recognized and activated. Later they will be fully realized. Now, this very day, we are to spread the good news. We are to be ambassadors of love, helping to birth saints who one day will stand together before our Father's throne, resurrected to eternal blessing beyond description.

The eventual number of saints in heaven is unknown. What's known is that the fields are ripe for harvest right now. What we must focus on is what the true saints of God always have had, an assurance of hope for tomorrow that enables a willingness today to be "living sacrifices" on behalf of the coming Light. Our daily prayer must be: "Let me live as a clear reflection of the coming God so that others may see and also find hope. Our gracious Father, show us the Light coming over the horizon of these troubled days. Reassure us that a gracious place is being prepared for us in that great beyond. Make us holy, that is, fit us now to show Jesus Christ to others even as we are learning ourselves to really live *in and by God's Spirit*."

---

[10] David Bundy, in the *Wesleyan Theological Journal*, 1988.

The details of what lies ahead are not ours yet to know. We live in the dim light of the already-not-yet, the dawning rather than the high noon of God's realized reign. In the meantime, may we keep singing the inspired words of Fanny Crosby:

> Blessed assurance, Jesus is mine!
> Oh, what a foretaste of glory divine!
> Heir of salvation, purchase of God,
> born of his Spirit, washed in his blood.
>
> Perfect submission, all is at rest,
> I in my Savior am happy and bless'd;
> Watching and waiting, looking above,
> Filled with his goodness, lost in his love.

God's kingdom has been inaugurated in Christ and now is coming alive in our midst through his Spirit. Jesus has come and the ministries to which we are called are those of his Spirit. The holy God intends a holy people united on a holy mission while on their way to a holy home. There's real spiritual life to be had now, a more excellent way to be pursued, a church to unite, and a world to save. Jesus has gone on to prepare our eventual homes and left us with a large assignment and his empowering Spirit.

The whole creation one day will be set free from its slavery to corruption. God will then be "all in all" (1 Cor. 15:28). Until then, while we serve and journey on in this world, our prayer should be:

> Take my life, and let it be,
> consecrated Lord to Thee.
>
> Take my moments and my days,
> let them flow in ceaseless praise.
>
> Take my hands, and let them move
> at the impulse of Thy love.
>
> Take my feet, and let them be
> swift and beautiful for Thee.[11]

---

[11] Lyrics by Frances Ridley Havergal.

Recent Resources

The Holiness tradition of Christian faith has been socially active and prophetic for many generations. For instance, found in the book *The Holy River of God* (Callen, 2016) is a sampling of recent and instructive statements on a range of important social topics, including:

> *Holiness Manifesto*
> *Fresh Eyes on Holiness*
> *A Call to Full Participation*
>   (women in ministry)
> *Gracefully Engaging the LGBT*
>   *Conversation*
> *Human Trafficking*

For classic and recent books on the several dimensions of Christian holiness, visit the web sites of the co-publishers of this present book, Emeth Press and Aldersgate Press, publishing arm of its parent body, the Wesleyan Holiness Connection. See:

> *HolinessAndUnity.org*

Also visit the web site of the Wesleyan Theological Society, especially for the hundreds of detailed articles in its *Wesleyan Theological Journal* on numerous subjects of interest to layperson and scholar alike.

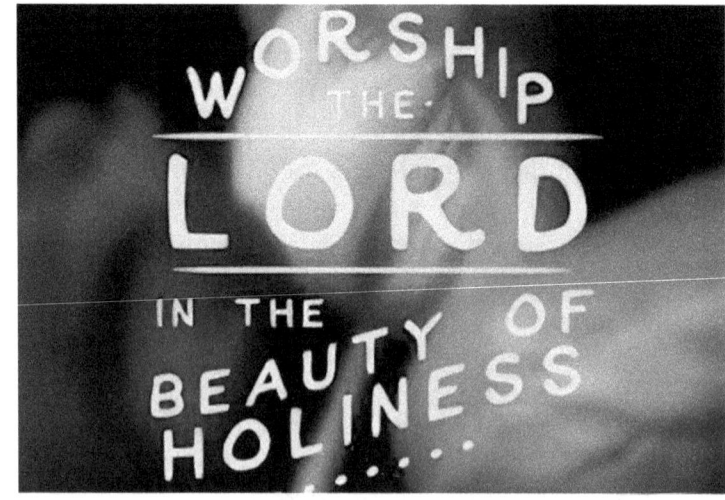

Books Referenced

Benson, Bob and Michael, *Disciplines for the Inner Life* (Word Books, 1985).
Bonhoeffer, *Dietrich, Letters and Papers from Prison* (SCM Press, 1953).
Briscoe, Stuart, *The Apostles' Creed* (Harold Shaw Publishers, 1994).
Brown, Kevin, and Michael Wiese, *Work that Matters* (Aldersgate Press, 2013).
Brueggemann, Walter, *The Unsettling God* (Fortress Press, 2009).
Callen, Barry L. and James North, *Coming Together in Christ* (College Press Publishing, 1997).
_____, *Radical Christianity: The Believers Church Tradition in Christianity's History and Future* (Evangel Publishing House, 1999).
_____, *The Wisdom of the Saints* (Warner Press, 2003).
_____, *Discerning the Divine: God Through Christian Eyes* (Westminster/John Knox, 2004).
_____, *Authentic Spirituality* (Baker Book House, 2002, rev. ed., Emeth Press, 2006).
_____, *Caught Between Truths: The Central Paradoxes of Christian Faith* (Emeth Press, 2007).
_____, *The Prayer of Holiness-Hungry People: A Disciple's Guide to the Lord's Prayer* (Francis Asbury Press, 2011).
_____, *Beneath the Surface* (Emeth Press, 2012).
_____, *Catch Your Breath! Exhaling Death and Inhaling Life* (Aldersgate Press, 2014).
_____, editor, *The Holy River of God* (Aldersgate Press, 2016).
_____, *Heart of the Matter* (Emeth Press, 2011, rev. ed. 2016).
_____, *God As Loving Grace* (Evangel Publishing, 1996, Wipf & Stock, 2018).

_____, *Faithful in the Meantime* (Evangel Publishing House, 1997, Wipf & Stock, 2018).

_____, *The Jagged Journey* (Aldersgate Press, 2018).

_____, with Steve Hoskins and Jonathan Powers, *A Year with Rabbi Jesus* (vol. 1, Emeth Press, 2021, vol. 2, 2022).

_____, *The Living Dead: Fantasy and Fear, Holiness and Hope* (Cascade Books, 2023).

Chilcote, Paul, *Praying in the Wesleyan Spirit* (Upper Room, 2001).

Collins, Kenneth J., *The Theology of John Wesley* (Abingdon Press, 2007).

Coppedge, Allen, *Portraits of God: A Biblical Theology of Holiness* (InterVarsity Press, 2001).

DeYoung, Kevin, *Hole in Our Holiness: Filling the Gap Between Gospel Passion and the Pursuit of Godliness* (Crossway, 2012).

Du Mez, Kristin Kobes, *Jesus and John Wayne* (Liveright Publishing Corp., 2020).

Finlayson, R. A., *The Holiness of God* (Pickering and Inglis, 1955).

Hines, Samuel G., with Curtiss Paul DeYoung, *Beyond Rhetoric* (Judson Press, 2000).

Greathouse, William, *Love Made Perfect: Foundations for the Holy Life* (Beacon Hill Press of Kansas City, 1997).

Gutierrez, Gustavo, *A Theology of Liberation* (Orbis Books, 1973).

Harkness, Georgia, *Foundations of Christian Knowledge* (Abingdon Press, 1955).

Harriman, Hubert, and Barry Callen, *Color Me holy!* (Aldersgate Press, 2013).

Heath, Elaine, *Five Means of Grace: Experience God's Love the Wesleyan Way* (Abingdon Press, 2017).

Henderson, D. Michael, *John Wesley's Class Meeting: A Model for Making Disciples* (Evangel Publishing, 1997).

Howard, Randy, and Tony Richie, *Pentecostal Explorations for Holiness Today* (Cherohala Press, 2017).

Jones, E. Stanley, *Abundant Living* (Abingdon-Cokesbury, 1942).

_____, *Song of Ascents* (Abingdon Press, 1968).

Kinlaw, Dennis, *The Mind of Christ* (Francis Asbury Press, 1998).

_____, *Lectures in Old Testament Theology* (The Francis Asbury Society, 2010).

Knight, Henry H., III, *Anticipating Heaven Below* (Cascade Books, 2014).

Kraybill, Donald B., *The Upside-Down Kingdom* (Herald Press, 2011).

Leclerc, Diane, *Discovering Christian Holiness: The Heart of Wesleyan Holiness Theology* (Beacon Hill Press of Kansas City, 2010).

Levison, Jack, *An Unconventional God* (Baker Academic, 2020).

Maddox Randy L., *Responsible Grace* (Abingdon Press, Kingswood Books, 1994).

Mannoia, Kevin W., and Don Thorsen, eds., *The Holiness Manifesto* (Eerdmans, 2008).

_____, *Masterful Living* (Aldersgate Press, 2015).

Massey, James Earl, *Concerning Christian Unity* (Warner Press, 1979).

_____, *Views from the Mountain*, Callen and DeYoung, co-eds. (Aldersgate Press, 2018).

Metaxas, Eric, *Bonhoeffer: Pastor, Martyr, Prophet, Spy* (Nelson Books, 2020).

Mitchell, T. Crichton, *Charles Wesley: Man with the Dancing Heart* (Beacon Hill Press of Kansas City, 1994).

Moltmann, Jürgen, *The Living God and the Fullness of Life* (Westminster John Knox, 2015).

Mulholland, M. Robert, Jr., *Shaped by the Word* (Upper Room, 2001).

Outler, Albert in *The Wesleyan Theological Heritage*, Oden and Longden, eds. (Zondervan, 1991).

Peterson, Eugene, *Practice Resurrection* (Wm. Eerdmans, 2010).

_____, *The Hallelujah Banquet* (Waterbrook, 2021).

_____, *On Living Well: Wisdom for Walking in the Way of Jesus* (2021).

Pinnock, Clark H., *A Wideness in God's Mercy* (Zondervan, 1992).

_____, *Flame of Love* (InterVarsity, 1996).

Ranier, Thom S., *Becoming a Welcoming Church* (B & H Publishing, 2018).

Raymond, Jonathan S., *Social Holiness: The Company We Keep* (Aldersgate Press, 2018).

Rohr, Richard, *Falling Upward* (Jossey-Bass, 2011).
Sanders, Cliff, *The Optimism of Grace* (Mid-America Christian University, 2020).
Seamands, Stephen A., *Holiness of Heart and Life* (Francis Asbury Press, 2022).
Snyder, Howard A. *The Radical Wesley & Patterns of Church Renewal* (InterVarsity Press, 1980).
Stafford, Gilbert W., *Theology for Disciples* (Warner Press, 2012).
Stewart, James S., *The Gates of New Life* (Charles Scribner's Sons, 1940).
_____, *Walking with God*, Gordon Grant, ed. (Regent College Publishing, 1996).
Strong, Douglas M., *"Holiness and Eccentricity,"* in Callen and Thorsen, eds., *Heart & Life* (Aldersgate Press, 2012).
Thorsen, Don, and Kevin Mannoia, eds., *The Holiness Manifesto* (Eerdmans, 2008).
_____, and Barry Callen, eds., *Heart & Life: Rediscovering Holy Living* (Aldersgate Press, 2012).
Thurman, Howard, *Jesus and the Disinherited* (Beacon Press, Boston, 2022 ed.).
Vickers, Jason E., *Minding the Good Ground: A Theology for Church Renewal* (Baylor University Press, 2011).
Virtue, David, *The Seduction of the Episcopal Church* (J2B Publishing, 2019, Kindle ed.).
Wainwright, Geoffrey, *Doxology: A Systematic Theology* (Oxford University Press, 1980).
Williamson, Clark, *A Guest in the House of Israel* (Westminster/John Knox, 1993).
Wynkoop, Mildred Bangs, *A Theology of Love: The Dynamic of Wesleyanism* (Beacon Hill Press of Kansas City, 1972, 2015).
Yoder, John Howard, *The Politics of Jesus*, 2nd ed. (Eerdmans, 1994).

www.ingramcontent.com/pod-product-compliance
Lightning Source LLC
Chambersburg PA
CBHW051944160426
43198CB00013B/2288